How to
PREPARE A
BUSINESS PLAN

How to PREPARE A BUSINESS PLAN

Edward Blackwell

KOGAN PAGE

First published in Great Britain in 1989 by
Kogan Page Limited, 120 Pentonville Road, London N1 9JN
Reprinted 1989

British Library Cataloguing in Publication Data

Blackwell, Edward
    How to prepare a business plan.
    1. Great Britain. Small firms.
    Management – Manuals
    I. Title
    658'.022'0941

    ISBN 1–85091–513–X
    ISBN 1–85091–514–8 Pbk

Typeset by The Castlefield Press Limited, Wellingborough, Northants.
Printed and bound in Great Britain by
Biddles Ltd, Guildford and King's Lynn

Contents

Acknowledgements

Grateful thanks are due to: The Executive Committee and the Director, Graham Sanger, of Macclesfield Business Ventures for their encouragement and support; my fellow Counsellors at MBV, whose brains I have shamelessly picked; John Rosthorn, former Director of MBV, for his valuable help and criticism; Jeremy Howarth for help with Example 7; the National Westminster Bank plc for permission to use its Cash Flow Forecast forms; and my wife, Hildegard, who has tirelessly typed out the text, corrected the spelling and grammar and is responsible, in general, for such readability as the book has.

Introduction

Starting a new business venture is like going into a tropical forest on a treasure hunt. There are rewards to be won, both in material wealth and personal satisfaction, but there are dangers lurking and you can easily lose your way.

This book is written not only to help you convince your financial backers that you will succeed and come back with a bag of gold, but also to help you write your own guidebook for the journey. The author has himself spent 40 years on foot among the trees, both in small business on his own account and as a guide and adviser to others.

Before beginning work on your business plan or your cash flow forecast, you would do well to ask yourself two vital questions:

What do you really want out of the business?
The answer to this question will fall into two parts.

The monetary rewards are obviously important. Set yourself a target. If anything less than a million pounds would be a bitter disappointment, then a million is what you are aiming for. If anything above £150 a week would give you cause for a major celebration, put that down as your target.

However, money is not all you are in business for. What else? Are you a born 'loner', anxious to be free from the constraints of a company set-up? Or someone with a yen to organise his own well-structured corporation? Would freedom to design your own products make your life worth living? Or do you just want to feel useful? Your strategy should reflect your own personal ends.

Think, too, about the time-scale. Are you determined to make a quick fortune and retire to *la dolce vita* or to a life of good works? Or, conversely, are you so fascinated by some aspects of what other people call 'work' that you would happily carry on as long as there is breath in your body?

Just jotting down what you hope to achieve will have begun to give shape to your plan. Next you must ask yourself questions about your resources, both mental and material. Consider your temperament and the talents you will bring to the business and how they will affect your planning.

Are you an outgoing sort of person, able to get on with and influence your fellow men and women? If so, the marketing side of business – finding out what people want and selling it to them – is likely to be your strong suit; but, with that same temperament, you may find you are not very happy or at your most efficient alone in an office and working out costs or struggling with the books. You may not possess, either, the 'toughness' required to deal with employees who do not perform. You might decide, therefore, against trying to run a production-led business or saddling yourself with the bookkeeping.

If you are the creative type but shy and inclined to worry, you would do well to base your business on design and innovation. Having to sell the goods yourself would doubtless prove a trial, and the problems of a production line, controlling the stock, etc, could give you more sleepless nights than you would care to contemplate. Can you make a living by selling your designs and inventions? If so, then concentrate on exploiting your undoubted talents to that end.

In classical times the entrance to the temple of Apollo at Delphi carried the inscription 'Know Yourself'. This admonition should be taken to heart by every business man and woman. Others may live happily with illusions about themselves; the small business person cannot!

The primary material resource you will want, of course, is money. Whether you need a few hundred pounds to start in business as a second-hand clothes dealer or a hundred thousand to set up a factory, it just has to be there, and a good deal of it must be yours. In the very small business, a rough rule of thumb is that you (or your family and friends) will have to produce half; and the other half is often very hard to come by. I believe that your chances of raising the extra finance will be greatly improved if your business plan and cash flow forecast are prepared along the lines laid down in this book.

What feature of your product or service will give you the all-important edge over your competitors?
Is your product or service:

1. An entirely new idea?
2. An improved version of something that already exists?
3. Cheaper than the others?
4. More reliable as to delivery or after-sales service?
5. More readily available to local customers?

In writing your plan, both for your own guidance and to reassure your financial backers, you must show that your personal objectives and your resources (both mental and material) are in accord with the strategy you will adopt to exploit the particular feature of your product. This harmony is a major key to success, and careful planning will help you to achieve it.

In this book I have not been content simply to write a set of rules and precepts. I have included several examples of business plans and cash flow forecasts. None of these is to be regarded as an ideal. They represent types or patterns which I consider appropriate and acceptable in each case for the size and type of business under consideration. I do not claim that the facts on which they are based are reliable, but I hope the way in which the imaginary writers of the plans have outlined their sometimes fanciful schemes will prove amusing as well as instructive.

Chapter 1
Writing a Business Plan

Business plans are required whenever money is to be raised, whether from a bank, a finance house, or a provider of equity capital.

To you, your business is of supreme interest and importance; to the bank or fund manager, your plan is but one of many that come across his desk. So you must win his approval and keep his interest. To do this:

- be clear
- be brief
- be logical
- be truthful
- back up words with figures wherever possible.

Clarity

The person reading your business plan is busy, often has other problems on his mind, and is consciously or unconsciously judging you by the way in which you express yourself. Therefore:

- keep your language simple
- avoid trying to get too many ideas into one sentence
- let one sentence follow on logically from the last
- go easy on the adjectives
- tabulate wherever appropriate.

Brevity

If the banker or manager gets bored while reading your stuff, you are unlikely to get the sympathetic hearing you deserve. So prune, and prune again, keeping in only the essentials of what your reader ought to be told. Lush descriptions are out.

Logic

The facts and ideas you present will be easier to take in and make more impact if they follow one another in a logical sequence. Avoid a series of inconsequential paragraphs, however well phrased. Also, make sure that what you say under one heading chimes in with all you have said elsewhere.

Truth

Don't overstate your case.

Figures

The banker or investor reading your plan is numerate; that is, he thinks in terms of numbers. Words will not impress him unless they are backed by figures that you have made as precise as possible. So try to quantify wherever you can.

Designing the business plan

The layout of your business plan can help greatly in keeping the reader interested. Above all, the information you give must follow a logical pattern. You could present your material in the sequence shown here, using headings, so that the reader can survey your plan and find his way without difficulty.

1. A brief statement of your objectives
2. Your assessment of the market you plan to enter
3. The skill, experience and finance you will bring to it
4. The particular benefits of the product or service to your customers
5. How you will set up the business
6. The longer-term view
7. Your financial targets
8. The money you are asking for and how it will be used
9. Appendices to back up previous statements, including especially the cash flow and other financial projections
10. History of the business (where applicable).

The above list can be added to, of course, if the people who will read your business plan have a special interest to which you should address yourself. For instance, public authorities are concerned to know the effect on local unemployment: write a special and prominent section to tell them about it.

Deciding how much to write

In all business plans something, however brief, should be noted on each of the items listed above. How much you put into each section should be in proportion to the size and scope of your project as the reader of your plan will see it. A busy bank official will not want to read through pages of material if he is being asked for no more than a few hundred pounds. On the other hand, he will not be impressed if, when asked to lend £100,000, he is given only a sentence or two on the aspect that interests him most.

Getting down to it

Careful writing of your business plan will give you a better insight into your own business.

You have a marvellous project; you have a shrewd idea that there is a market for it; you have obtained a good deal of advice from experts and have done sums to calculate your hoped-for profits, your cash flow and the money you need to raise. So, when you get the finance, you will be ready to go. Or so you believe! But it is odds-on you still have homework to do. Now is the time to do it.

'Writing,' said Sir Francis Bacon, 'makes an exact man.' There is nothing so effective in testing the logic and coherence of your ideas as writing them out – in full. As the future of your business depends in large part on your ideas working in a logical and coherent way, now is the time to subject them to this test.

How do I set about it?
Taking the sections numbered above one by one, make notes under each heading of all you have done or expect to do. For example, regarding Section 2, what do you really know about the market you want to enter? Have you done enough market research? Who are going to be your customers? How many will there be? How will you contact them? How will you get your goods to them?

Or, when it comes to Section 5, have you a clear, concrete picture of what you will actually do to 'get the show on the road'?

Write it all out! Perhaps you would like to adopt the following method: taking a large sheet of paper for each of the above sections, note down the facts relevant to each of them; then sort them, test for truth and coherence and arrange into a logical pattern.

You will prune hard when you come to write the document itself. In the meantime you will have organised your ideas, you will have noticed gaps and weaknesses, and the business is bound to go the better for it.

Tackling each section

1. *The brief statement*
   This should be to the point. Just something to show the reader what it is all about. Say what you do in one sentence. In a second sentence state how much money you want and what you want it for.

2. *The market*
   When you come to the main body of your document, start with the section which is most likely to impress your reader. The majority of people lending money believe that what makes for success in business is finding and exploiting a large enough market. So, as a rule, the 'market section' should be the one with which you lead off.

   Though your product may be the best since the invention of the motor car and you may have the talents of a Henry Ford, you will get nowhere if there is no call for your brainchild or you lack the means of projecting your product into the market. The person reading your plan will know this only too well, and he will want to find out whether you are aware of these facts and how well you have done your homework. Your market research is crucial.

   Note that where figures are given, and they should be given freely, the authority for the figures should be quoted. If your figures can be checked, this will promote confidence.

3. *The skills, experience and resources of the persons involved*
   A lender or investor will want to know the track record of the persons to whom he is entrusting his own or his clients' money. Therefore, you must give a fairly full account of your own business career and those of your co-directors or partners. School and academic histories are hardly relevant. Past achievements and technical qualifications, on the other hand, are.

   Of almost equal importance is the degree of your financial investment. You cannot expect others to risk money in an enterprise to which the founders themselves are not financially committed in a big way.

4. *The benefits of your product*

This is the most difficult part about which to comment because it is the section in which you are likely to wax most enthusiastic. Human progress depends on new ideas, and people with good ones need all the support they can get. That having been said, you must face the fact that only a minority of innovations can be made commercially viable. Your banker or financier has probably seen hundreds of absolutely brilliant ideas come to naught, and for all kinds of reasons. So this is the section you will have to write most soberly.

A famous American writer – a writer, not a businessman – once said that if you made a better mouse-trap, all the world would beat a path to your door. Any successful businessman could have told him that simply making a better product is only one step on the way to success, and not even the first or the most important step.

Do not get too disheartened. You have, you believe, a first-class product and, as you demonstrated (in Section 2, above), the market for it is there. What you must do now is to persuade your reader that your product is a good one and that it will have the edge to help you exploit the opportunities set out in Section 2.

Stick firmly to hard fact! 'Puff' sentences, such as 'This is the best widget-grinder on the market and will be the cheapest too', cut very little ice. Show, with figures, why it is the best and why it should be the most expensive. If you have some independent test results, say so, and give at least a summary of them in an appendix. A few genuine figures are worth a page of adjectives, on which, as was stated earlier, you must go easy.

Information that could be included in this section:

- a brief description of the product or idea
- how it works
- why it is better than its rivals
- any independent appraisal (with details in an appendix).

5. *The method*

By this time your reader will have a clear idea of your market, your skills and the customer benefits of your product. What he wants to know is whether you are going to set about things in a sensible and workmanlike manner. Tell him what he should know in terms that are as concrete as possible.

(a) First of all, how do you propose to market the product or

17

service? Will you have your own sales force? What will you do about publicity and advertising? How will you 'target' your sales drive? Under what terms will you sell? When will you be starting on all this? Give a firm time schedule, if possible.

(b) It will promote confidence if you outline your 'management structure'. If you have partners or colleagues, who will be responsible for what? How do you intend to keep the various sections in touch with one another? Will you have management meetings once a week? Once a month? Or only when there is a desperate crisis? What about keeping employees abreast of what is going on and what is expected of them?

(c) Outline the production methods you will adopt at the start of the project. Write something, briefly, about the premises you will use. A sentence, or possibly two, will tell of the plant and machinery. You may need a workforce. State how many people you will need at the beginning and later, as sales increase. What will be the capacity of the initial set-up?

(d) The office is your next concern. As a skilled engineer or a keen salesman, you may be impatient of all the paperwork. However, to convince your reader that your business will not descend into chaos or grind to a halt, tell him who will see to it that it does not. Who will make sure that the letters are answered in your absence? Who will look after the books? Answer the phone? Process orders? Invoices? Who will chase up debtors? Have you assessed the amount of work which will need to be done in this department?

(e) Your reader will also want to know how you will control and monitor the business financially. The smallest business needs to know at all times what its cash position is. As soon as there are those who owe you money, or to whom you owe money, it will be necessary to keep a regular check. Your banker or investor will know that many an otherwise good business has come to grief through lack of elementary financial controls. Larger businesses will need more elaborate controls. Ensure not only that you have made the necessary arrangements, but that your investor knows you have given this aspect proper regard. Any good accountant should be happy to advise you.

6. *The longer-term view*

So far, so good. You have explained how you will get your

project off the ground and how it will run during the start-up period. Now the banker or investor will want to know how he stands for the future.

Some enterprises are essentially short term. Some should continue to be very profitable over a longer period. Some will be slow-growing, and their financial needs can be met out of profits. Others will have to accelerate fast, and they will need further injections of capital on a pre-planned basis. Your financial backer will want to know your thoughts on all these points.

If yours is a project to exploit some 'trendy' idea, the backer will expect some assurance that, if the fashion were to change, he could be paid out of liquid funds and not be locked into unamortised fixed assets, ie fixed assets whose cost has not yet been recovered out of profits and which would be difficult to sell. In general, he should be told how you see the market over two years, over five years, and in the long term. Also, what you propose to do about potential competition.

The hope is that you will be highly successful. This may well mean that, sooner or later, despite excellent profits, you will need more capital. Here is where you show that you are prepared for this.

Sales forecasts for new ventures are very difficult to make. Trying to predict sales for more than a year ahead is even more difficult, and the experts themselves almost always get it wrong. Usually, such is human nature, they are over-optimistic. But this is no reason for not making the best estimate you can. You have to have some target on which to base your plans.

In this section you can also write about any developments – new products or new markets – in which you hope to involve your company in the future.

7. *Use of the funds*

Now that your reader knows that you have a good product, that there is a market for it, and that you know how to run the business in an efficient way, you should explain, in fair detail, why you need his money and how you will spend it.

Emphasise how much money you and your colleagues are investing. No one is going to risk his money on your project if you are not substantially committed.

Having added up the sums you are putting in and all that you are hoping to raise, list the items you will be spending the money on, such as:

- patents
- land and buildings (give some details)
- plant and equipment (specify major items)
- cost of publicity for the initial launch
- working capital (reference to cash flow forecasts)
- reserve for contingencies.

8. *Financial targets*

Although your hopes and plans for financing your business will be set out in all the cash flow forecasts, etc, which you will attach as appendices, it will be helpful if you give a brief summary now of the salient points. No matter how small the business, you will be expected to show:

- the expected turnover for the first year
- the expected net profit for the first year
- how much of the loan will be paid off in one year
- when you expect to pay off the loan entirely
- what you hope for in the second year (when payments from the Enterprise Allowance Scheme, if any, will no longer be coming in).

You do not have to show that the business will make a profit in the first year. Your banker knows that many businesses make a loss initially and still go on to succeed. If you show that you can expect to achieve profitability in the long term, your banker should be prepared to go along with this.

However, if you are raising equity capital (see page 109), there are other considerations. Most equity investors expect to be with you a long time. They are interested in capital gain and, if available, dividends. The additional information they will want is:

- the rate at which you expect profits to grow
- what your dividend policy will be
- what you and the other directors will be taking out of the business before the equity holders' share in the profits
- what plans or ambitions you have (if any) to sell out, to buy them out, or to go on to the USM (Unlisted Securities Market), a junior branch of the Stock Exchange.

A typical cash flow forecast form as supplied by the National Westminster Bank is shown on pages 22–3. Some of the items listed may not apply in your case, and there may be items missing which you would wish to include. Just cross out or blank out non-relevant items and substitute those you want. For example, you might, perhaps, eliminate 'Corporation tax' or 'Dividend' and fill in 'Motor expenses' instead.

9. *The appendices*

What you have said so far should have told your reader all about your project. You have now to add documentation to convince him that you have done your homework properly and that you can show good evidence for what you have said. Last and most important will be the detailed financial forecast. This will vary from the relatively simple cash flow forecast on a form supplied by your bank to an elaborate 'business model' prepared by a professional accountant.

The financial projections are the real meat of the whole business plan. A great deal of information should be given, especially in the cash flow forecast. Chapter 2 is devoted to this subject.

Other appendices could be copies of any documents that will support what you have said previously. They might include:

- accurate summaries of any market research, either your own or what has been professionally carried out
- photocopies of local newspaper articles describing a need for a service you propose to provide
- pictures of your product or products
- copies of your leaflets or other promotional literature
- the results of any testing of your product, especially if it has been done by an independent organisation.

The general outline given so far is intended as a guide for those seeking funds for a new enterprise. If you want finance to expand an existing business or to take over an existing shop, the principles will remain the same, but you will need to write an additional paragraph or page, preferably at the beginning of your business plan, to do with:

10. *The history of the business*

This section should be brief, factual, and based on the audited trading results. At least three years' results should be shown, if possible, as well as the last balance sheet. Reference may be made to such fuller comment, explanation and plans for change as may be given in later pages, eg under 'Marketing' or 'Management'.

National Westminster Bank PLC						**Cashflow Forecast For**
Branch						name of company, firm etc

Enter month						
Receipts	Projected	**Actual**	Projected	**Actual**	Projected	**Actual**
Sales – Cash						
Sales – Debtors						
Loans						
Other receipts						
A Total receipts						
Payments						
Cash purchases						
To creditors						
Wages and salaries (net)						
PAYE/NIC						
Capital items						
Rent/rates						
Services						
Professional fees (D. Gray)						
Bank/finance charges						
Loan repayments						
VAT (net)						
Corporation tax, etc						
Dividend						
B Total payments						
Opening bank balance						
Add to B if overdrawn Subtract from B if credit						
C Total						
D Closing bank balance (Difference between A&C)						

For the period

| From | | To | | | | | |

						Total	
Projected	Actual	Projected	Actual	Projected	Actual	Projected	Actual

Illustration 1

The history should also tell of any major changes in ownership or management, of significant market alterations or
trends – in other words, it should mention any important
happening that has affected the business over the past few
years.

Chapter 2
Simple Cash Flow Forecasts

What is a cash flow forecast?

To those who are venturing into business for the first time, the prospect of having to draw up a cash flow forecast can be intimidating; but the banks will demand one when a loan is sought for even the smallest of one-man enterprises. This is because they believe it will give them at least some idea as to whether and when they are likely to get their money back.

The cash flow forecast sets out, usually in monthly columns, the sums you expect to receive by way of sales, Enterprise Allowance, etc, and compares this inflow of money with the payments you will be making for stock, for materials, for overheads, for equipment, and the money you will have to take out of the business for living expenses. An example is shown on pages 50–51.

It is not a forecast of the profitability of the business, but merely a guess as to whether, in the short term, more cash will come in than goes out. That is not necessarily the same as profitability. On the one hand, although your profit margins might not be adequate to cover overheads and write off the cost of equipment, your cash flow could be good enough to pay the bank back its money while you were losing yours. On the other hand, there are profitable businesses (ie their net assets are growing nicely) which are what is called 'cash hungry'. They may be making fine profits, but all the cash they take in, and more, is needed to increase stock or give credit to an ever larger number of customers. So the bank, far from getting its money back, will be lending more and more. Sooner or later the bank will call a halt, and you may have to close your business, despite its underlying profitability.

Is a cash flow forecast of any real use?

A cash flow forecast which is badly drawn up is clearly of little use. It serves merely as a snare and a delusion. Unfortunately, the projected figures in your forecast will depend on the reliability of your crystal ball in foretelling your sales figures. You may improve the accuracy of those figures by conscientious market research, by getting advance orders (or at least firm promises), but you will still be peering into an uncertain future.

However, if the sales figures appear reasonable and conservative, and if the cash flow forecast has been well and logically drawn up, the bank will be able to 'take a view' as to whether it can lend the money (and get it back again without having to sell up your house and furniture – a step even the toughest bank manager is loth to take).

To persuade the bank or building society to lend you the money you need is, of course, the primary purpose of a cash flow forecast. It has, however, some other very important uses.

Actually producing a well thought out forecast fulfils the same function as writing a well prepared business plan. It will sharpen up your ideas. It will make you aware of the effect on your bank balance of the decisions you take in your planning, eg the amounts to be spent on advertising, your terms of sale (very important for cash flow), whether or not to buy your own transport, etc. Giving thought to your cash flow is a very worthwhile exercise. Try drawing up several forecasts, each based on rather different assumptions of sales and expenditure. The few hours you spend could prove the most profitable of your life!

Even the smallest business is more likely to do well if its owner keeps a close eye on its financial progress, comparing what he hoped and planned for with what is actually happening. In business jargon this is called 'budgetary control'. In your cash flow forecast you will have an invaluable little tool when you come to set up your own small-scale budgetary control. So don't tear it up once the bank has seen it. Use it. Most of the banks now appreciate the value of their cash flow sheets as budgetary control documents and provide adjoining columns for 'forecast' and 'actual'. If every month, and immediately after the month-end, you fill in all the figures in the 'actual' column, you will get a quick indication of anything that is going wrong, together with strong hints as to where to target any remedial action.

Principles to observe when filling in a simple cash flow form

1. Enter the more certain figures first
2. Make every entry in the month in which the cash and cheques are handed over
3. All entries must be inclusive of VAT where applicable.

Start by entering those payments of which you are certain (or almost certain):

the rent — in the actual months when it must be paid
the rates — for each month when they must be paid
HP payments on any vehicles or machinery
loan repayments on any fixed-term loan you have agreed or hope to agree
wages of any regular employees
the sums you will have to draw from the business to live on
any other payments you expect to have to make if you know the amounts.

Now also enter the sure regular receipts, such as:

Enterprise Allowance payments
Rents from any sub-let.

The next items are more difficult. They are overhead payments, the amounts of which are not yet certain because the invoices have not been received. These will include:

gas and electricity bills
telephone bills
advertising and publicity costs
petrol and other motor expenses
stationery and printing
postage and packaging
insurances
repairs and renewals
etc (the etceteras will depend on the nature of your business).

These items cannot be predicted with any great accuracy but, if you have done your homework, you should be able to make reasonable estimates. Enter them, of course, for the months when you will have to pay them. 'Repairs and renewals' are a special case. They are by their very nature uncertain, both as to amount and timing. Make a good guess as to the yearly cost and divide this into four quarterly payments.

The next thing to do is to enter the initial receipts and payments – those once-and-for-all transactions that get you started. The receipts could include:

fixed loans from the bank
loans from family or friends
money of your own which you pay into the business account
    after the date of start-up
grants.

The payments could include:

capital payments for the lease
machinery and equipment
initial licence fees
legal fees
installation costs
office equipment
starting stock
advertising to launch the product.

Remember that the cash flow forecast is deemed to start on a specific day – usually the first of the month. Any payments made or moneys received before that date must be ignored. You are writing a cash flow, not a profit and loss account.

Many of these initial costs will be paid in the first month and should be entered in the appropriate spaces for that month. However, you may get extended credit for, say, 30 days or six weeks for some items. Enter them for the months in which they will actually be paid.

Most of your figures will have been entered now. But you still have the difficult part to do. You must tackle the sales side. This is a matter of putting hard figures to the faith you have in your product. You know in your bones that the product or service will sell. But how well? And how soon will the money start to come in? You will have done some market research even if, as a potential window cleaner, you have done nothing more than call on the neighbours to find out how many will pay to have their windows cleaned. Use all the information you have gleaned about your market; link this with the amount of time you will be able to devote to selling, and you should be able to make some sort of educated guess at the turnover you can expect once you have got going properly.

But your sales will not be the same month by month, surely. For one thing, you will probably take a month or two to reach the sales target you have set yourself. Adjust your figure to allow for this possibly slow build-up.

Pre-start orders for those fortunate enough to have them from friends or from business contacts will give you a splendid start and help enormously with the cash flow for the first month or two, but they are easy orders, and there may well be a downturn in later months when you have to start relying on new sales to new contacts.

Now, you may not be in the business of making chocolate Easter eggs or Mother's Day bouquets, but there is almost certain to be some seasonal element in your business. It may be nothing more than that you, as a self-employed worker, go away for an annual holiday. But build this seasonal factor into the sales profile.

If yours is a 'cash only' business, you can enter your monthly sales figures straight on the 'cash sales' line on the chart. But, if you are going to give credit to your customers, the cash flow will have to be adjusted for this. That share of the sales that is for cash (or cheques) will still be entered on the 'cash sales' line, but the credit sales will suffer a time-lag before they are entered on the 'cash from debtors' line. This time-lag will depend on two factors:

- your 'terms of sale' as regards time allowed for payment
- your customers' adherence to those terms.

Incidentally, do make sure that your terms of sale are stated clearly on your quotations. Simply to put them on your invoice has no legally binding force.

If your terms of sale decree payment in 30 days and half your customers observe them, then you will receive payment for 50 per cent of this month's credit sales next month, and 50 per cent in the month after next. Likewise, if you give 60 days' credit and two-thirds pay within the time given them, you will get payment for 66 per cent of this month's sales the month after next, and 33 per cent in three months' time.

There is also the question of the discounts you offer in order to obtain prompt payment. These, too, affect the cash flow.

There are innumerable variations of both simple and sophisticated trade terms that can be offered. You will adopt the ones that suit your market best, but with the strong proviso that only the cash-rich can afford to give credit without offering discounts for prompt payment.

Let us take some examples, assuming monthly sales of £1,000 per month:

1. Terms – Net 30 days (half pay on time).

	May £	June £	July £	August £
May sales paid	0	500	500	
June sales paid		0	500	500
July sales paid				500
Totals	0	500	1000	1000

2. Terms – Same, but you give 2½ per cent discount for immediate payment (half take the discount, the rest split as before).

	May £	June £	July £	August £
May sales paid	487	250	250	
June sales paid		487	250	250
July sales paid			487	250
August sales paid				487
Totals	487	737	987	987

3. Terms – 60 days' credit, no discount (two-thirds pay on time).

	May £	June £	July £	August £
May sales paid	0	0	667	333
June sales paid		0	0	667
July sales paid			0	0
Totals	0	0	667	1000

4. Terms – Same as for 3, but you give 5 per cent discount for immediate payment (half take the discount, the rest split as before).

	May £	June £	July £	August £
May sales paid	475	0	333	167
June sales paid		475	0	333
July sales paid			475	0
August sales paid				475
Totals	475	475	808	975

You have now settled the cash sales line and the 'receipts from debtors'. The time has come to settle the purchase of 'materials' (or 'goods for resale', as the case may be). You are going to run a tight ship, of course, as far as purchases are concerned. You have seen too many businesses go down the river through bad buying. You will avoid, therefore, buying more than you need for current production or sales, however tempting the bulk purchase discount. Excellent!

So your purchases will be strictly related to your sales figures. As far as possible you will buy in the month what you will use – or sell – in the month. If you are in a trading business (exceptions will be dealt with below), your purchases for the month will equal your sales, less the average mark-up. If yours is a manufacturing business, you must take into consideration the 'lead time of production', that is to say, the actual time it takes to make the goods up to the time of invoicing them, and your purchases must be adjusted accordingly.

Let us deal with the retail or pure trading business first. Here, to the best of your ability, you are buying to sell in the same month. So the purchases will equal the sales, less the average trade discount. If you have to pay cash for goods, that is that. But, very likely, you can get at least a month's credit from suppliers, so sales will lead purchases.

Let us take some examples, assuming in all cases a mark-up of 33.3 per cent on selling price:

1. All sales for cash. All purchases for cash. Sales a steady £5,000 per month, except in August and December.

	May £	June £	July £	Aug £	Sept £	Oct £	Nov £	Dec £	Jan £
Cash sales	5,000	5,000	5,000	2,500	5,000	5,000	5,000	10,000	5,000
Purchases	3,333	3,333	3,333	1,666	3,333	3,333	3,333	6,666	3,333
Cash flow	1,667	1,667	1,667	834	1,667	1,667	1,667	3,334	1,667

2. As before, but 30 days' credit is received for half the purchases.

	May £	June £	July £	Aug £	Sept £	Oct £	Nov £	Dec £	Jan £
Cash sales	5,000	5,000	5,000	2,500	5,000	5,000	5,000	10,000	5,000
Purchases									
this month	1,667	1,667	1,667	833	1,667	1,667	1,667	3,333	1,667
last month	0	1,667	1,667	1,667	833	1,666	1,666	1,666	3,333
Payments to creditors	1,667	3,333	3,333	2,500	2,500	3,333	3,333	4,999	4,999
Cash flow	3,333	1,667	1,667	0	2,500	1,667	1,667	5,001	1

This pattern of payments and receipts, which is by no means uncommon, is worth a little study. Note the sudden cash shortage which appears in August and January. These are the months in which heavy payments are made and, especially in August, the cash receipts are relatively low. If money is not held back from, say, June or December to meet the requirements of August and January, the business could well be in difficulties. Any self-employed man or woman should keep a cash flow forecast and update it regularly just to watch out for such problems.

Let us return to our examples:

3. As 1, but half the sales are on 30 days' credit and half the customers pay on time.

	May £	June £	July £	Aug £	Sept £	Oct £	Nov £	Dec £	Jan £
Total sales	5,000	5,000	5,000	2,500	5,000	5,000	5,000	10,000	5,000
Credit sales	2,500	2,500	2,500	1,250	2,500	2,500	2,500	5,000	2,500
Cash from creditors									
last month's		1,250	1,250	1,250	625	1,250	1,250	1,250	2,500
two months ago			1,250	1,250	1,250	625	1,250	1,250	1,250
Cash sales	2,500	2,500	2,500	1,250	2,500	2,500	2,500	5,000	2,500
Total cash received	2,500	3,750	5,000	3,750	4,375	4,375	5,000	7,500	6,250
Payments to creditors	3,333	3,333	3,333	1,666	3,333	3,333	3,333	6,666	3,333
Cash flow	−833	417	1,667	2,084	1,042	1,042	1,667	834	2,917

It is interesting to see, in the last example, that the month of highest sales produces one of the lowest cash flows, whereas the month of lowest sales produces the second highest cash flow. This is by no means an unusual phenomenon.

The choice of trade terms can seriously affect your cash flow, not only in your paper forecasts but for deadly earnest in real life. You will have to decide what are the best terms, appropriate to your situation for both buying and selling, that you can reasonably expect to obtain; then apply them to your cash flow forecast.

It is assumed that you will be able to relate your purchases to sales on a month to month basis, as should be possible in most cases. However, when there is an element of 'fashion' involved, this close relationship between sales and purchases does not apply.

For example, in the dress or shoe trade, there are summer styles and winter styles. All buying for the summer is done in the winter for delivery and invoicing in, say, March/April. A similar time-lag applies to the winter trade. In this type of business, what is not sold in one season is unlikely to be worth hanging on to for the next-but-one. Hence the end-of-season 'Sales', when goods are sold for whatever they will fetch, sometimes for less than cost. Anything that could become dead stock must be turned into cash at almost any price.

Let us take, for example, a firm which buys £80,000 worth of goods during the year, evenly split between summer and winter. The mark-up on cost is 100 per cent. The firm expects to sell 85 per cent during the season, the remainder to go into the 'Sales' at cost. The cash pattern will be:

	Cash received £	Payments £	Cash flow £
April	17,000	40,000	−23,000
May	17,000		17,000
June	17,000		17,000
July	17,000		17,000
August (Sales)	12,000		12,000
September	17,000	40,000	−23,000
October	17,000		17,000
November	17,000		17,000
December	17,000		17,000
January (Sales)	12,000		12,000

The principle of relating purchases of materials to expected sales also applies to a manufacturing company. Random buying is out. Avoid above all the temptation to buy more than you know you will need in the short term just because of a very favourable discount you are offered.

Your purchases must relate to your production schedule, which in turn must relate to your forecast of sales.

The above has been highly simplified by taking two seasons of five months each, ignoring February and March, and by assuming that profit-earning sales are spread evenly.

If you have been following my suggestions and filling in the figures on your cash flow forecast, it ought to be nearly complete. Only one or two tidying-up operations remain to be done.

The first, but by no means the most important, is to provide a 'contingency fund' or a 'Murphy's Law (if anything can go wrong it will go wrong) Allowance'. It is a provision you would do well to make to cover all those unforeseen misfortunes that crop up to plague the businessman. It is not there to cover shortfalls on items for which you have budgeted above, but to protect you, to some extent at least, against the wholly unexpected. Calculate it as a small percentage, perhaps 2½ per cent of turnover. Treat it as VATable and enter it monthly.

The second and much more important operation is to allow for VAT, if you have registered for it. You have presumably included VAT in the entries you have made so far; it now remains to calculate the quarterly payments you will have to make to the Customs and Excise (or, if applicable, the repayment claims).

You are probably taking advantage of the proposals in the Finance Act of 1987 and paying VAT on a cash basis. Though you can opt to pay monthly, VAT is usually paid quarterly, the month after the end of the quarter. For example, if your last quarter ended on 30 April, then in May you will pay VAT for the months of February, March and April.

You begin by adding up the sales, including VAT, for the first three months, multiply by 15 and divide by 115. This will give you your VAT 'output'. Next, you add up the VATable items of expenditure for the same three months and do the same calculation. This gives you your VAT 'input'. The difference will be the VAT you will pay in the fourth month.

Note. The following expenses are not VATable:

> rent
> rates
> wages and National Insurance
> insurance
> gas
> bus and train fares
> bank charges
> electricity
> postage
> licence fees
> books, etc.

Note, too, that VAT on motor cars (other than vans and lorries) is not recoverable, and there is no VAT on second-hand cars.

You will remember that in a previous paragraph, you were cautioned against including in your cash flow forecast any expenditure paid for before day 1. However, the VAT you have paid as part of such expenditure does come into the calculations because you can recover it, and it will be part of the 'inputs' that you claim for in the first quarter. So, the pre-start-up VAT must be added in when you do the first quarter's calculations.

You will calculate in the same way for the second and the third quarters, but the fourth quarter's VAT will not be part of this cash flow forecast. This is because it will not be paid until the first month of the second year (where it will have to appear if you are doing a second-year forecast).

If you are borrowing from the bank, you still have the bank interest to deal with. If, however, you decided that it would be more economic to raise the necessary money by remortgaging your house with your building society, the interest will be taken care of in the repayment arrangements and does not form a separate item. But let us assume that you are borrowing from the bank.

The loan can take one of two forms. It can either be a loan for a fixed term, with fixed repayment arrangements, or it can be in the form of an overdraft facility. In the first case, the loan is sure, the repayments are fixed, and the interest can be calculated readily with reference to the prevailing bank rate. On the other hand, you will have to pay interest on the whole of the outstanding loan even if your current account is well in the black.

The overdraft facility, although it has the advantage of only incurring interest on the amount ourstanding at any time, is less certain, as the bank can withdraw or reduce it at any time. However, it is particularly appropriate as a means of covering temporary fluctuations in cash flow due to, say, seasonal patterns of buying. Most banks are prepared to negotiate a mixture of fixed loan and overdraft to meet the individual case.

With all the figures for cash in and cash out now entered, you can add up the 'ins' and the 'outs' for each month and work out the effect on your bank balance. Each bank has its own Cash Flow Forecast form, and you will have to do the calculations according to the bank's method. In principle, you start with the current account balance on the day you begin business; you add 'cash in' and take away 'cash out'. Your new end-of-the-month balance, of course, becomes the starting balance for the next month.

Your cash flow forecast is now ready to be pinned to your business plan and handed in to the bank.

A cash flow forecast as outlined above is probably as complicated a production as can be expected from someone lacking professional training and access to a computer. It will just about do when a loan of up to two or three thousand pounds is wanted. But if tens of thousands of pounds are required, then a more sophisticated document will have to be prepared, preferably a full business model, with forecast profit and loss accounts and balance sheets. This is a task which should be put into the hands of professionally qualified accountants and is not covered here.

At the end of Chapters 3 and 5 examples are given to demonstrate, step by step, how a simple cash flow forecast is prepared.

Chapter 3
The Very Small Business

If you want to set up a one-man business or go into partnership with a friend, you may wonder why you should go to the trouble of writing a formal business plan. Why not just fill in the bank's own cash flow form and explain all else at an interview?

There are two good reasons why you should write out a proper plan: first, as pointed out in Chapter 1, because it will help you to better understand your business and its problems; and, second, because of the nature of bank procedures.

It may be that your bank manager is a friendly type who really wants to help the small businessman, but he is working under conditions imposed from above. He is an expensive member of a big bureaucracy. No doubt he would like to be the father-figure of the TV ads, dispensing benevolent advice to all his customers. In practice, however, he spends much of his time in administration, dealing with the problems of those below him in the hierarchy and reporting to those above. He also has to promote and advertise the bank locally. His time for actually dealing with customers is not unlimited. Naturally enough, he is expected to concentrate on the best-paying customers – the bigger ones. One cannot reasonably hope for anything else. The bank is not a charity.

Therefore, except in the smaller branches, it is highly likely that your application for a loan will be dealt with, in the first instance, by a junior, though the manager may make the final decision. Now, there are problems in dealing with a junior, even when 'manager' appears as part of his title. For one thing, a junior is only given power to say 'No'. He will have no power to say 'Yes'. Almost certainly his function is to act as a filter, so that the manager will not have to waste time on doubtful cases. Moreover, his junior status may mean that as yet neither his good judgement nor his conscientiousness has been proved. Therefore you must spare no effort to ensure that it is your application which goes forward to the manager himself. A well-written business plan will not only be impressive in itself, it will save the junior having to write up his own report on your project. This could give you a big advantage.

Once you have decided to write the plan, you will have to decide how much to say. Facing the fact that the bank will see you as small fry, you will be well advised to limit the main part of the plan to two typed A4 pages, or three at the very most. You can add appendices, such as those listed on page 21, which could include a fuller account of any technical details you feel should be added; also, of course, the cash flow forecast. You do not have to write as much as if you were starting a larger concern, such as those described in the later chapters.

However, even in a two-page document, you must cover the points listed in Chapter 1, namely:

1. What it is all about (often one sentence will do)
2. How big your market is and what is the competition
3. If you have already started, what progress has been made
4. Your own skill and experience
5. How your product or project compares with others
6. How you will get your act together
7. The longer-term view
8. How much turnover and profit you can expect
9. The money you need and why.

The same principles apply as listed on the first page of Chapter 1. On the following pages you will find examples of business plans appropriate when applying for a loan of a few hundred pounds. I will also go through the stages of filling out a bank's cash flow forecast form.

Example 1

My name is Alexander Battersby. I am a skilled joiner by trade and I wish to borrow £500 to set up in business on my own.

The market for my services
My uncle, George Battersby, who has been a self-employed joiner for 20 years, has decided to retire and will let me have his list of customers and contacts and sell me his tools. In the last year or two he has been doing about £850 worth of work a month. I am sure that, with extra energy, I can increase this to at least £1,000 per month and that this will involve less than 20 hours per week actually working on the job.

I have also been talking to the managers of two of the local DIY shops. Both tell me that at least one in ten of DIY projects started by householders runs into trouble and that many people, having started a job, wish they had never begun. If I advertise myself as being willing to put things right, I am sure I could get a lot of profitable work.

About myself
I am aged 27 and a fully trained joiner, with nine years' experience since completing my apprenticeship.

I have also had experience in plastering and decorating and have some skill in tiling and bricklaying.

I am attending a course in design at the local technical college.

I am married with one son.

How I will set about my business
I cannot use my own house as a base, but my Uncle George will let me use his old premises at his house until I can find suitable ones of my own. I will pay him £5 a week rent.

I shall have to buy a van. To do this I will sell my car. I can get a good second-hand van for £1,400, and I will get £900 for my car after paying off the HP.

Advertising in the first month in the local paper will cost £100. To emphasise continuity with my uncle, I will trade as Battersby & Co.

A lady called Doreen Gray runs a bookkeeping and secretarial service. I have been strongly recommended to use her services to keep my paperwork in order. This will cost £50 per month.

I also intend to give written quotations for every job to avoid arguments afterwards.

I shall insure against third party risks.

The future
If the business reaches a turnover of much more than £22,000 I shall have to register for VAT. For the present, most of my customers will be private people who will not be able to recover the VAT I should have to charge. My ambition is to get more work from builders and others who are registered for VAT themselves, so that in the long term I will no longer have to rely on private customers.

How I will use the money
I have £950 of my own in a building society. I am asking for an overdraft facility of £500. The money will be used as follows:

	£
Van	500
Tools	375
Licences and Sundries	150
Advertising	100
Working capital	230
	£1,355

Paying back the money
As will be seen from the enclosed cash flow forecast, I do not expect to use the whole of the overdraft, but I have asked for enough to cover any normal misfortune. I intend to pay back any overdraft within the six-month period, even if the sales are less than expected.

The information given by Alexander leaves some questions unanswered, but it is quite clear that he knows what he is about, that he has thought over the problems he will face in going it alone. He realises that his knowledge of bookkeeping is limited. If Doreen Gray is even moderately competent, she will keep him clear of the paperwork muddle that defeats so many self-employed people. And on the basis of this plan, most bank managers should look upon Alexander as a good risk for a small loan.

But there is still the cash flow forecast to prepare. Let's go through the steps as they apply to Alexander.

For purposes of illustration we shall assume that Alexander Battersby is applying to the National Westminster Bank for a loan and, in preparing his cash flow forecast, is using the form depicted on pages 22–3.

Alexander realises that certain items under 'Payments' on this form will not apply in his case. Like most small businesses, his is not, nor will it be, a limited company. He will not pay corporation tax (or, until his profits have been determined, any income tax). Nor will he pay a dividend. Alexander will insist on cash payment, so all his sales will be 'Sales-Cash'. He will not have to fill in the 'Sales-Debtors' line.

The lines for 'HP/leasing repayments' and 'VAT' do not apply to his business, as he has no HP debts and is not registered for VAT. So all these lines can be blanked out and used, if needed, for something else.

Now, following the principles laid down in Chapter 2, Alexander will have to fill in the blanks for the certain payments he will be making. They will be:

1. Rent/rates — Rent, including rates, is payable weekly at £5 per week, ie approximately £22 per month, starting in month 1.
2. Payments to Doreen Gray — at £50 per month, and as she will be paid each month for the work she did the previous month, the first entry will be made in month 2.
3. Drawings — Alexander and his family have to live, and he decides he must draw £420 per month from the business, starting in month 1.

Note. Many people going into business for the first time ask what wages they can pay themselves on PAYE. This question reveals a misunderstanding of the tax status of someone who is self-employed or running his own business as a sole trader or in partnership. Unless you form a limited company, which is usually inadvisable, you cannot pay yourself 'wages' which are subject to PAYE. You will be taxed at the end of the year on the profits you have made, and you cannot affect those profits and the tax payable thereon by paying yourself 'wages' or 'salary'. In fact, the amount of income tax payable will not be affected by how much or how little you draw out of the business for yourself. (You can, however, if your spouse works in the business, pay him or her a wage, and this will be subject to PAYE.)

It is strongly recommended that you keep your business payments and your private or household payments strictly separate. Adopt a system of making regular drawings from the business account and never pay for private expenditure out of the business directly. In most cases it pays to have two separate bank accounts (or a bank account and a building society account), one for business, the other for private and family use. Keeping the two apart will save you no end of trouble and confusion.

Getting back to Alexander Battersby and his cash flow forecast, there are the other ongoing overheads (as listed in Chapter 2):

4. *Electricity* — Alexander believes he will have to pay his uncle approximately £15 per quarter to cover his share of the bill. Enter for 'Services'.

5. *Telephone* — Alexander has a telephone at home and estimates that he ought to contribute £20 every quarter from the business account. Add £20 to the 'Services' figure in March and June. (Alexander must pay these sums into his private account in the designated months.)

6. *Advertising* — It is hoped that the business will grow by word of mouth after advertisement in the local press and a distribution of leaflets that will take place at the start. However, Alexander will budget for £50 every three months starting in May.

7. *Petrol and other motor expenses* — £30 every month, with an extra £100 every quarter to cover oil, repairs, etc.

8. *Stationery and printing* — After the initial expense, £5 per month is expected to cover this.

9. *Insurances* — These are paid in the first month: £300.

10. *Repairs and renewals* — Alexander does not think he will need to spend much on repairs for some time, other than perhaps to the motor van. However, he agrees it would be wise to allow £12 per month to cover 'contingencies'.

You can now see (Illustration 2, pages 44–5) how Alexander's cash flow forecast will look at this stage.

Alexander himself will now have a good idea of what he will need to earn in order to cover his monthly overheads and feed and clothe his family. He reckons his earnings will have to average at least £650 per month.

The next step will be to fill in the start-up payments and receipts. You will remember that Alexander listed his start-up costs.

The van and tools – together £875 – will be entered as 'Capital items' and the others as 'Licences and Advertising'. ('Working capital' is not entered. This item will be dealt with later.)

On the first day of trading Alexander will withdraw the £950 from his building society account and pay it into his new business account at the bank. The amount will be entered as 'Capital introduced'.

The cash flow forecast will now look like Illustration 3, pages 46–7.

Next, the sales figures must be tackled. The estimate of sales in this case is made relatively simple by the fact that Alexander is sure he can carry on where his uncle left off – with basic sales of £850. In the first month the sales figure will be less, however, because he will not have been able to finish a biggish job and will not, therefore, be paid for it until later. Alexander believes that by April his sales campaign – leaflets and personal visits – will have paid off and his sales increase. The cash sales, he hopes, will be:

January	February	March	April	May	June
£780	£850	£850	£900	£950	£950

These figures are entered on the 'Sales-Cash' line.

Next, the purchase of materials must be dealt with. Alexander estimates that the cost of materials will account for about 12 per cent of the amount charged on bills sent out, as a good deal of his work will consist of repairs. At a turnover of £850, this works out at £102.

Uncle George has arranged with some of his suppliers to continue to extend a month's credit on supplies when Alexander takes over. Half Alexander's materials will be obtainable on this basis. So his 'Cash Purchases' line will look like this:

January	February	March	April	May	June
£51	£51	£51	£54	£57	£57

The 'To Creditors' line will show:

0	£51	£51	£51	£54	£57

Now Alexander has nearly completed his cash flow forecast and can add up the columns and rows – preferably in pencil at this stage. The sheet should look like Illustration 4 (pages 48–9).

The bank balance lines remain to be filled in. As Alexander is starting at 9 o'clock on day 1 with nothing in the bank – his own £950 to be paid in later that day – he enters 'nil' as his opening balance and works out the closing balance as instructed on the Nat West form. He finds he will be overdrawn by £230 at the month end, and this is the figure he uses as 'working capital' in the business plan paragraphs above.

The closing bank balance for one month becomes the opening bank balance for the next month, so Alexander will only need one more item to complete the form. The bank official has told him what the standard bank charges will be, and Alexander realises that there will be interest for two months. A quick calculation shows him that his bank charges and interest for the first quarter will amount to approximately £35, so he enters this figure in the space for the appropriate month and adjusts his additions. The sheet should now look like Illustration 5 (pages 50–51).

When the bank balance lines have been filled in, the cash flow forecast is complete, and Alexander notes with pleasure that he stands a good chance of having nearly £700 in the bank by the end of June. This is, of course, not his profit for the six months; on the one hand, he has drawn out £2,520 and, on the other, he still owes – to his suppliers and Doreen Gray, among others – over £100.

Although he is determined never to be overdrawn by more than £230 if he can help it, Alexander has shown prudence in asking for an overdraft facility of £500. This amount should cover him against the unexpected crises that can occur in business when least expected.

In Chapter 10 you will see how Battersby & Co got on and how Alexander used this forecast as a simple budgetary control.

National Westminster Bank PLC   **Cashflow Forecast For**

Branch   6 High Street, Ourtown   name of company, firm etc

Enter month	January		February		March	
Receipts	Projected	**Actual**	Projected	**Actual**	Projected	**Actual**
Sales – Cash						
Sales – Debtors						
Loans						
Other receipts						
A Total receipts						
Payments						
Cash purchases						
To creditors						
Wages and salaries (net)						
PAYE/NIC						
Capital items						
Rent/rates	22		22		22	
Services					35	
Professional fees (D. Gray)			50		50	
Bank/finance charges						
Advertising						
Motor expenses	30		30		130	
Insurance	300					
Sundries (& Licences)			5		5	
Drawings	420		420		420	
Contingencies	12		12		12	
B Total payments						
Opening bank balance						
Add to B if overdrawn Subtract from B if credit						
C Total						
D Closing bank balance (Difference between A&C)						

For the period

Alexander Battersby   From Jan 198-   To June 198-

April		May		June		Total	
Projected	**Actual**	Projected	**Actual**	Projected	**Actual**	Projected	**Actual**
'							
22		22		22			
				35			
50		50		50			
		50					
30		30		130			
5		5		5			
420		420		420			
12		12		12			

Illustration 2

National Westminster Bank PLC					Cashflow Forecast For
Branch 6 High Street, Ourtown					name of company, firm etc

Enter month	January		February		March	
	Projected	Actual	Projected	Actual	Projected	Actual
Receipts						
Sales – Cash						
Sales – Debtors						
Loans						
Other receipts	950					
A Total receipts						
Payments						
Cash purchases						
To creditors						
Wages and salaries (net)						
PAYE/NIC						
Capital items	875					
Rent/rates	22		22		22	
Services					35	
Professional fees (D. Gray)			50		50	
Bank/finance charges						
Advertising	100					
Motor expenses	30		30		130	
Insurance	300					
Sundries (& Licences)	150		5		5	
Drawings	420		420		420	
Contingencies	12		12		12	
B Total payments						
Opening bank balance						
Add to B if overdrawn Subtract from B if credit						
C Total						
D Closing bank balance (Difference between A&C)						

	For the period		
Alexander Battersby	From Jan 198-	To June 198-	

April		May		June		**Total**	
Projected	**Actual**	Projected	**Actual**	Projected	**Actual**	Projected	**Actual**
22		22		22			
				35			
50		50		50			
		50					
30		30		130			
5		5		5			
420		420		420			
12		12		12			

Illustration 3

National Westminster Bank PLC						Cashflow Forecast For
Branch 6 High Street, Ourtown						name of company, firm etc

Enter month	January		February		March	
	Projected	Actual	Projected	Actual	Projected	Actual
Receipts						
Sales – Cash	780		850		850	
Sales – Debtors						
Loans						
Other receipts	950					
A Total receipts	1730		850		850	
Payments						
Cash purchases	51		51		51	
To creditors			51		51	
Wages and salaries (net)						
PAYE/NIC						
Capital items	875					
Rent/rates	22		22		22	
Services					35	
Professional fees (D. Gray)			50		50	
Bank/finance charges						
Advertising	100					
Motor expenses	30		30		130	
Insurance	300					
Sundries (& Licences)	150		5		5	
Drawings	420		420		420	
Contingencies	12		12		12	
B Total payments	1960		641		776	
Opening bank balance						
Add to B if overdrawn Subtract from B if credit						
C Total						
D Closing bank balance (Difference between A&C)						

For the period

Alexander Battersby | From Jan 198- | To June 198-

April Projected	April Actual	May Projected	May Actual	June Projected	June Actual	Total Projected	Total Actual
900		950		950		5280	
						950	
900		950		950		6230	
54		57		57		321	
51		54		57		264	
						875	
22		22		22		132	
				35		70	
50		50		50		250	
		50				150	
30		30		130		380	
						300	
5		5		5		175	
420		420		420		2520	
12		12		12		72	
644		700		788		5509	

Illustration 4

49

National Westminster Bank PLC					Cashflow Forecast For	
Branch 6 High Street, Ourtown					name of company, firm etc	

Enter month	January		February		March	
Receipts	Projected	**Actual**	Projected	**Actual**	Projected	**Actual**
Sales – Cash	780		850		850	
Sales – Debtors						
Loans						
Other receipts	950					
A Total receipts	1730		850		850	
Payments						
Cash purchases	51		51		51	
To creditors			51		51	
Wages and salaries (net)						
PAYE/NIC						
Capital items	875					
Rent/rates	22		22		22	
Services					35	
Professional fees (D. Gray)			50		50	
Bank/finance charges						
Advertising	100					
Motor expenses	30		30		130	
Insurance	300					
Sundries (& Licences)	150		5		5	
Drawings	420		420		420	
Contingencies	12		12		12	
B Total payments	1960		641		776	
Opening bank balance	NIL		−230		−21	
Add to B if overdrawn Subtract from B if credit						
C Total	1960		871		797	
D Closing bank balance (Difference between A&C)	−230		−21		53	

For the period

Alexander Battersby		From Jan 198-		To June 198-			

April		May		June		**Total**	
Projected	**Actual**	Projected	**Actual**	Projected	**Actual**	Projected	**Actual**
900		950		950		5280	
						950	
900		950		950		6230	
54		57		57		321	
51		54		57		264	
						875	
22		22		22		132	
				35		70	
50		50		50		250	
35						35	
		50				150	
30		30		130		380	
						300	
5		5		5		175	
420		420		420		2520	
12		12		12		72	
679		700		788		5544	
53		274		524			
626		426		264			
274		524		686			

Illustration 5

Example 2

We, Rosemary Rambler and Muriel Tonks, whose business address is 14 Church Road, Witherspool PS3 7HT, are applying for a loan of £7,500 to promote the business of designing and selling garden statuary.

The market

With the increase in tourism in the UK and the need for improved and smarter hotels, gardens and parks, we have found there is a wide and expanding market for good quality garden and hotel statues. Marble and bronze are too expensive and cast iron or mock stone lack aesthetic appeal; but the recent development by the Tolpuddle College of Advanced Technology of the new Alloy 237B has made it possible to cast statues to attractive appearance at a marketable price.

We have had one finished statue produced and maquettes made of four more. With these we have approached five hotel groups and also 40 private individuals. Great interest has been shown. Paradise View Hotels plc have given us a firm initial order for 20 statues at £650 each plus VAT and, we believe, will buy more when the initial order has been completed, ie in 12 months' time. We also have orders for four statues from private buyers.

Our sales effort so far has been limited but the results have been very encouraging. We estimate that there is a potential market for 10,000 statues of this type. We ought to be able to obtain at least 10 per cent of the market, as we are first in the field with high-quality designs and products. 1000 units sold over five years implies sales of £650,000 plus VAT.

Ourselves

Rosemary Rambler, aged 32, to be Artistic Director and in charge of production.

1973–76: Attended the Brize-Norton College of Art. 1976–79: Worked in the atelier of Art Slivowitz, the sculptor, in Paris. 1980–81: Unemployed. 1982–87: Lecturer in sculpture at Ourtown Polytechnic. Has been commissioned to do scenery design for several theatre productions, including the famous musical *Titus Andronicus* at the London Palladium. Also designed the frieze on the new Bladderwick Town Hall.

Muriel Tonks, aged 23, to be responsible for marketing and sales in addition to all office work and financial arrangements.

After attending Ourtown Polytechnic classes in Art for two years, went into commercial life as a management trainee at Ourtown Home Stores Ltd; at present employed there as Assistant Buyer. Also attending Ourtown College of Further Education classes in Business Management.

The product

The advantages of Alloy 237B are that the metal is both cheaper and has a lower melting point than bronze, making it easier to cast.

The metal is supplied by Vintage Metals Ltd of Birmingham, and we have a contract with Stanislavski Foundry Ltd to cast two statues per month at a price to remain fixed for one year. The cost to us per standard statue, approximately 5 ft × 3 ft, including metal and casting, will be £345 plus VAT.

We shall concentrate on producing five models during the first year. Models can be ordered from maquettes as follows:

1. The Copenhagen Mermaid
2. The Mannekin Pis
3. Rodin's 'Thinker'

4. A Lion Rampant
5. A Bust of Winston Churchill

This selection was made to cater for a wide variety of tastes. Casting problems made us reject two otherwise popular suggestions, Cellini's 'Perseus' and a group of the 'Two Ronnies'.

Our short-term plan
Our statues will be produced by what is known as the 'lost wax' method. This involves making full-size plaster models of each statue from which the foundry can proceed to make the final metal statues.

One metal statue has been cast satisfactorily and is ready to be invoiced to the customer. Two further full-scale plaster models have been delivered to the foundry ready to be cast. Rosemary's first priority will be to complete the last two full-scale models which, with part-time help from Muriel and some casual work from students from the College in their spare time, should take 10 weeks. In the meantime the foundry will be casting from the existing full-scale models.

We have acquired suitable premises on Church Street, Witherspool at a rent of £1,500 a year which will provide a studio for designing new models and a workshop for adding the final touches to each statue and for packing and despatch. There is also space suitable for an office and a showroom for the display of small-scale models or maquettes.

We do not believe that, at least during the first year, we shall need to employ other than occasional casual labour.

The limiting factor is the Stanislavski Foundry's lack of sufficient capacity for casting more than one statue per fortnight. The foundry has committed itself to expansion, however, and a letter, attached hereto as Appendix A, attests to this fact.

Being essentially a marketing and design partnership, we propose to spend heavily on publicity and advertising in our first year. Muriel will concentrate on selling our products. We shall rely on mail shots, telephone sales and personal visits to large hotel groups and other likely enterprises. We propose to buy an Amstrad computer and use it not only as a word processor for our letters, invoices, etc, but to set up a database of actual and potential customers.

We have received very useful help from the Witherspool Enterprise Agency and have gratefully accepted its offer of continuing support and advice.

We shall also consult regularly with our accountants, Messrs Belt & Braces of Ourtown.

In view of the fact that most of our customers will be commercial firms, we will register for VAT immediately.

The longer-term strategy
With a target of selling approximately 1000 units in five years, we are planning on a rapid expansion to an annual production of 400 units in the fifth year. Such expansion will involve:

1. Either a further substantial increase in capacity at the foundry we are using at present or a search for another firm able to take on the additional work.
2. An increase in our range of statues by the addition of perhaps four new models a year. Market research will determine what models will be designed.
3. Finding larger premises, probably in two years' time, and taking on more staff. We expect to employ three more skilled people within the five years and

at least one unskilled or semi-skilled person.

The financial situation
It has been agreed that the work already done, essentially by Rosemary, shall be valued at £4,000, this to include the one finished statue ready for sale and invoicing. A family loan to Muriel of £4,000 will be her contribution to the partnership assets. This will be paid into the partnership account on day 1.

The partners will then share profits and losses equally. A partnership deed is being drawn up by Messrs Manyana, Manyana & Holliday, solicitors.

The partners are asking for a fixed-term loan of a further £4,000, repayments to start after nine months and then by eight three-monthly instalments. In addition, an overdraft facility of £3,500 is requested.

Of our starting capital of £8,000, we shall spend £1,500 on a small second-hand car to be used mainly for sales visits. We shall also have to equip an office and buy hoists, etc to help with packing and despatch. Here is how we plan to use the £8,000:

Car	£1,500
Office equipment	1,000 (including VAT)
Alterations to premises	500 (including VAT)
Equipment	600 (including VAT)
Working capital	4,400
	£8,000

The need for working capital will be heavy in the first year, due in part to the limited capacity of the foundry. Messrs Stanislavski are installing additional capacity and have promised to do their best to speed up production. In our financial forecast we have not allowed for any increase in production over what the foundry has promised to achieve. In view of our sales potential, any increase in production would have a dramatic effect on our profits and cash flow.

The following documents are attached as appendices:

- letter from the Stanislavski Foundry Ltd
- photograph of our first statue
- schedule of overheads
- forecasts of profit and loss and cash flow

In these accounts we are 'capitalising' all expenditure on design and the making of moulds. We are writing it off as a charge against the cost of each statue produced, as can be seen in the profit and loss forecast.

In our second year we expect to sell a minimum of 140 statues, producing a profit as follows:

Sales		£91,000
Less Metal and casting	£48,300	
Moulds and design	2,400	
Overheads	12,300	
Wages	7,500	
Interest	300	
Depreciation	800	71,600
Profit		£19,400

A cash flow forecast was produced on the partnership's Amstrad computer. (See Illustration 6 on page 57.) Although it looks different from the one done on a bank form by Alexander Battersby, it does follow the basic principles laid down in Chapter 2.

There, you will remember, you were advised to begin by listing all the fixed amounts you knew you would have to pay, followed by those other charges, like electricity, that would be regular but unpredictable as to the precise amount.

Rosemary and Muriel's cash flow goes beyond this by including a complete schedule of all the overhead payments they expect to make, month by month. The amounts are entered here net of VAT. Some of the items will be free of VAT and some will be subject to VAT. Next the VAT on the VATable items is calculated. At the foot of each column are added up the non-VATable items, the VATable items and the VAT thereon, the total representing the overhead payments due for the month. (The figures are shown in Illustration 6.)

You will notice a thirteenth column on the right which has been used to estimate the various overhead payments relevant to the year which will not be paid until after the year end. Added to the monthly payments, this will give the total of overhead expenses that affect the year's profit.

Preparing an overhead schedule like this is a useful exercise for any small business man or woman. If he knows the total commitments for overheads for a year, then, by dividing by 12, he will know how much gross profit he must make each month just to cover the fixed overheads.

For instance, a retailer whose fixed overheads come to £6,000 a year will know that he must have £500 per month gross profit to cover them, and if his profit margin on sales is 25 per cent, then a turnover of £2,000 per month (nearly £100 per day) is needed for overheads alone. And this does not take into consideration any wages, any interest on capital, any depreciation or any profit for the owner himself.

Rosemary and Muriel also wanted to have some idea of the profit or loss they might make in their first year, so a profit and loss forecast was devised. (See Illustration 7 on pages 58–9.)

There is a line which represents the 'Fixed overheads', one-twelfth of the annual total excluding VAT. (Remember, if one is registered for VAT, VAT does not affect the profit and loss account.)

The 'Value of sales' line represents the invoiced value of the number of statues sold in the month.

The 'Metal and casting' figure represents the bought-in cost from the metal supplier and foundry for that same number of statues.

Rosemary and Muriel realised that in working out the cost of each statue they had to allow for the expenses incurred in making the design and in constructing the mould. They worked out the average cost per design plus mould and then divided the figure obtained by the number of statues they thought could be made from the mould before it wore out or the demand for that particular statue fell away. After careful consideration they decided on a figure of £20. One line in the profit and loss forecast represents this cost.

There is also a line for 'Interest' payable on their loan. And a line for 'Wages' – other than wages for design and mould making, which are included in the £20. Other than for making moulds, they do not expect to have to employ anyone during the first year.

The last item of expenditure is 'Depreciation'.

Next, Muriel prepared a cash flow forecast for the year. In this table all figures must include VAT, where applicable, as she is dealing with the actual movement of cash.

The 'Sales' line represents the actual receipts of money for the statues assuming they were paid for in the month after they were invoiced.

The 'Moulding materials and wages' represent the amounts actually spent on these items, as do the amounts for 'Overheads' – from the 'Overhead Schedule' – for 'Interest' and for 'Capital payments'.

There is a line for 'Drawings' representing what Rosemary and Muriel need as living expenses, and lines to show the cash they have borrowed and their own money which they have introduced. The 'Loan repayments' are also shown in their due time.

The VAT line is constructed by deducting the VAT on payments to suppliers, both of ongoing cost and overheads, and the capital payments, from the VAT charge to customers. The calculation is made quarterly, and payment is made in the month immediately after the quarter's end.

Note that, due to the heavy payments combined with a lack of receipts in the first month, Rosemary and Muriel will be able to claim a VAT repayment for the first quarter.

Rosemary Rambler and Muriel Tonks

Overhead Schedule

	Month 1	Month 2	Month 3	Month 4	Month 5	Month 6	Month 7	Month 8	Month 9	Month 10	Month 11	Month 12	Outstanding	Total
Rent	750						750							1500
Rates		40	40	40	40	40	40	40	40	40				400
Heat and light				200			200			200			200	800
Insurances (inc car)	825													825
Road fund licences			200											200
Bank charges				30			30			30			30	120
Telephone	100			250			250			250			250	1100
Advertising and printing	270	270	270	270	270	270	270	270	270	270	270	270	270	3510
Petrol etc	100	100	100	100	100	100	100	100	100	100	100	100		1200
Office and other sundries	25	25	25	25	25	25	25	25	25	25	25	25		300
Professional fees		250											600	850
Repairs and renewals			100			100			100			100		400
Contingencies	30	30	30	30	30	30	30	30	30	30	30	30		360
Total (ex-VAT)	2140	715	765	945	465	565	1695	465	565	945	425	525	1350	11565
VAT thereon	79	101	79	101	64	79	101	64	79	101	64	79	168	1159
Total Payments	2219	816	844	1046	529	644	1796	529	644	1046	489	604	1518	

Illustration 6

57

Rosemary Rambler and Muriel Tonks
Profit and loss and cash flow forecasts

Profit and Loss Account

	Month 1	Month 2	Month 3	Month 4	Month 5	Month 6	Month 7	Month 8	Month 9	Month 10	Month 11	Month 12	Total
Number of statues sold	1	3	3	3	4	4	4	5	5	6	6	6	50
Value of sales	650	1950	1950	1950	2600	2600	2600	3250	3250	3900	3900	3900	32500
less													
Metal and casting	285	855	855	855	1140	1140	1140	1425	1425	1710	1710	1710	14250
Models and design	20	60	60	60	80	80	80	100	100	120	120	120	1000
Overheads	964	964	964	964	964	964	964	964	964	964	964	964	11568
Interest	47	47	47	47	47	47	47	47	47	41	41	41	546
Wages													0
Depreciation	67	67	67	67	67	67	67	67	67	67	67	67	804
Profit	-733	-43	-43	-43	302	302	302	647	647	998	998	998	4332

Cash Flow Forecast

	Month 1	Month 2	Month 3	Month 4	Month 5	Month 6	Month 7	Month 8	Month 9	Month 10	Month 11	Month 12	Total
Receipts from sales		748	2243	2243	2243	2990	2990	2990	3738	3738	4485	4485	32893
Loans	4000												4000
Other receipts	4000												4000
Total receipts	8000	748	2243	2243	2243	2990	2990	2990	3738	3738	4485	4485	40893
Payments for:													
Metal and casting	0	983	983	983	1311	1311	1311	1639	1639	1967	1967	1967	16061
Moulding materials	460	460	57	57	230	230	57	57	230	230	57	57	2182
Ditto wages	60	120				60				60			300
Overheads	2219	816	844	1046	529	644	1796	529	644	1046	489	604	11206
Interest			141			141			141			123	546
Other wages													0
Drawings	500	500	500	500	500	500	500	500	500	500	500	500	6000
Capital payments	3600												3600
VAT				−721			194			381			−146
Loan repayments									500			500	1000
Total payments	6839	2879	2525	1865	2570	2886	3858	2725	3654	4184	3013	3751	40749
Balance	1161	−2131	−282	378	−327	104	−868	265	84	−446	1472	734	144
Bank balance	1161	−970	−1252	−874	−1201	−1097	−1965	−1700	−1616	−2062	−590	144	144

Illustration 7

Chapter 4
Buying a Retail Business

Britain is a nation of traders. Our financial system is in many ways geared for trading rather than for making goods. The 'money men' understand and sympathise with trading projects much more readily than with schemes for manufacturing.

This in itself harbours dangers for the person who wishes to open or buy a retail business. Britain is full of brilliant, aggressive traders: wholesale traders, traders in goods, traders in stocks and bonds. Whatever the commodity, there is a Smith, a Jones, a MacTavish, a Shah or a Patel busily trading in it, making use of all his skill and experience, and backed by a supportive financial system. The competition is terrific. It starts at the top. The enterprise and cut-throat ruthlessness of the great corporations filter down, affecting the small side-street shops and making the earning of a decent living very hard indeed.

Nevertheless, as a retailer you will probably get a relatively sympathetic hearing from the banker. He not only has an inherent understanding of trade, but there are two other reasons for his preference. The first is psychological. When a manufacturer goes bust, he does so pretty dramatically, and egg gets splashed on many faces. The failure of a shop is a much slower process as a rule – a steady descent into poverty and squalor. It goes almost unnoticed except by the victims.

The second reason for a banker's preference is based on the fact that it is often possible to sell even a moribund retail shop. If one man fails, another will be along, convinced that he can make a go of it. The British yearn to be shopkeepers and often possess not only a touching faith in their ability to run such a business, but quite often the cash as well, by way of redundancy money, to buy one, however derelict.

Be that as it may, the retailer presenting a business plan retains an in-built advantage in that the banker does know what he is talking about. It is highly unlikely that the banker is also a scientist or an engineer or has spent time in a factory. But he has been in a shop and knows what goes on there. So the retailer will have far less explaining to do. There will be no need to translate a lot of technical jargon. Furthermore, if he has been living in the area for more than a few months, the banker will almost certainly know the location of the shop in question and the pattern of trade. This should also cut down on the need for words.

'So why,' you will ask, 'should I write an elaborate business plan at all? Why not just send in the required cash flow forecast, copies of accounts, if any, supplied by the vendor, and a short covering letter?'

First, despite the understanding and sympathy many bankers feel for traders as against manufacturers, they do know that very many retail shops lose money. Experience has shown that even if the bank recovers its money, there is often very little left for the owner. Your banker is not an ogre. He will want to assure himself that you are not making a bad mistake but fully understand what it is you are proposing to undertake.

Second, the principle laid down in Chapter 1 applies with at least equal force to retail business. Writing a comprehensive business plan is the best way of ensuring that the strategy and tactics to be employed are well thought out and logical. There are more dangers and difficulties entailed in running a retail business than most people think.

Two questions require particular attention: What is the market for your goods, and what should your buying policy be?

1. The market

- Is there a sufficient market for your goods in the catchment area of your shop?
- What must your share of the market be to enable you to make a reasonable profit?
- How many pairs of feet will be passing your shop each day?
- How many of these will turn into the shop, ie become customers?
- How much will each customer have to spend to give you a reasonable annual profit?
- Are the 'multiples' getting an increasing share of the trade in your goods?

Questions like this must be asked and the answers entered in your business plan.

2. *Your buying policy*

If you have chosen the right site and the right type of goods to sell, the surest way of losing money is through bad buying. You must work out a sensible buying policy based on your expected monthly rate of sales and the ratio of stock to cost of goods sold. Set down that policy in your business plan. If you are going to employ an organised system of stock control – and you ought to do so – say so and give an outline of your methods. How often will you do a physical stocktaking? The more frequently you do one, the greater will be your stock control over your business.

There are, of course, other problems that a retailer may face, to do with employment of staff or security of tenure, for instance, but the two that are common to all retailing are choice of site and buying of stock. These are the two aspects of the business about which you must write a great deal in your business plan, no matter what type of retail operation yours is.

The first example of retail enterprise illustrates the unhappy position of someone whose education has failed to give him or her skills that are of economic value. He or she often turns to retail trade in a desperate hope of succeeding in self-employment.

Often it is the unskilled or semi-skilled man, having lost his job, who is in this position, but the example concerns Nicola Grant, aged 32, who has just been divorced and has two small children.

Example 3

Nicola Grant had been in touch with an agency listing small shops and businesses for sale and became interested in a grocery business about which she had been sent details.

The asking price of the business, including the lock-up property, was £42,500 'plus stock at valuation'. On further enquiry, she learned that the property itself was valued at £32,000, leaving £10,500 for goodwill and fixtures (not including the bacon slicer and fridge which, Nicola found later, were on HP). The estimated value of the stock was £16,000.

Nicola had been given a copy of a trading and profit and loss account for the year ending July 1986. It had been explained that the accountants, Messrs Edmund Gibbon & Co, had not yet completed those for 1986–87. The accounts for 1986 had the figures for 1985 alongside and looked like this:

Mr & Mrs Smith (Quality Food Shop)

Trading Account
Year ended 31 July 1986

	1986 £	1986 £	1985 £	1985 £
Sales		76,076		78,542
Stock at start	13,630		12,524	
Purchases	61,752		65,283	
	75,425		77,807	
Stock at end	15,780		13,630	
		59,645		64,177
Gross Profit		£16,431		£14,365

Profit and Loss Account
Year ended 31 July 1986

	1986 £	1986 £	1985 £	1985 £
Gross profit		16,431		14,365
less Wages and NIC	3,934		3,927	
Rates and insurance	792		750	
Heat and light	775		690	
Telephone	275		272	
Bags and wrapping	179		185	
Motor expenses	2,116		1,935	
Repairs	311		270	
Sundries	217		193	
Bank charges	45		50	
Accountancy	450		400	
Hire purchase	100		50	
		9,194		8,722
Profit for the year		£7,237		£5,643

Nicola was impressed by the increasing profit which, the vendors told her, was due to 'better buying'. When she said that she could not afford to buy the property, they offered to let it to her on a lease for £3,000 a year, 'tenant to pay all repairs, with an option to buy at a price to be agreed'.

Although £3,000 would be cut off the net profit, Nicola felt that £4,237 a year – or £80 a week – was still worth having, and she had always, since childhood, wanted to run a little shop. Some friends at a party told her that if she were to add more lines, such as wines and spirits, they would all buy from her, and the shop could be a 'little gold mine'.

She approached the bank and was given a sympathetic hearing, but was advised to go to the Ourtown Enterprise Agency for guidance in the drawing up of a cash flow forecast and business plan.

Nicola explained to the counsellor at the Agency that she had £4,000 saved up with a building society and that her father would lend her £9,000 more to set her up in business. As the goodwill, stock and fixtures would come to £26,500, she would have to borrow £13,500 from the bank, offering her home as security.

When the counsellor examined the accounts, his face took on a rather solemn expression. He suggested to Nicola that they draw up a list of what the overheads were likely to be the following year, with Nicola running the shop. Together they produced the following:

	£	
Wages	3,500	Nicola would still need part-time help
Rent	3,000	
Rates and insurance	825	
Heat and light	780	
Telephone	150	Nicola would be economical
Bags and wrapping	150	The shop was overstocked in these
Accountancy	450	
Repairs	350	Nicola agreed much needed to be done
Motor expenses	2,500	Nicola would still have to go to the cash and carry wholesalers
Sundries	225	
Hire purchase	250	The fridge had been acquired since the last accounts
Interest	2,025	£13,500 at 15%
Total	£14,205	

The counsellor pointed out that this level of overheads would leave Nicola with only £2,296 profit to live on – £44 per week – out of a gross profit as shown for 1986 (£16,431). Moreover, as the counsellor said, the turnover seemed to be going down rather than up, and it was doubtful whether in 1988 the 1986 sales could be maintained.

Nicola was horrified by these figures and, for a moment or two at least, she hated the counsellor for spoiling her lovely dream. There was no argument, however. Unless the turnover were to increase dramatically, there would be no real profit from the business. Nicola knew her party friends too well to believe that they would go out of their way to bring trade to her shop, and even if they did, their purchases would amount to no more than a pittance. The counsellor pointed out that to stock up with wines would cost money and there was no

65

guarantee of sales. In his opinion the business was hardly worth buying, and certainly 'goodwill' should not figure as an item in the price.

Nicola decided to make one further effort, however. She went back to see the Smiths and told them what the counsellor had said. They were outraged. They then 'confessed' to Nicola that they had taken £75 a week 'at least' out of the business before declaring their income for tax.

Nicola returned to give the counsellor this additional information, but he had 'heard that one before'. While it could have been just possible in 1985, when an extra £75 a week added to the turnover would have produced a gross profit of 22 per cent, such an addition to the 1986 figures would have produced a gross profit of 25.4 per cent, far beyond the average for a shop of that type.

Nicola took the point and, sighing, decided to abandon the project.

In the Introduction, the importance of having an 'edge' over the competition was emphasised. Unfortunately, finding an edge is often more difficult for the would-be shop owner than it is for the small manufacturer or someone in a service trade.

The large chain stores are so powerful in controlling the distribution of well advertised lines that it is impossible to compete with them on price. Competing on 'service', in the old sense of giving personal attention to customers, is of little real value except in the case of technical goods. Retail service these days means, for the most part, providing a large supermarket where a family with a working mother can do all the regular shopping for a fortnight under one roof and take it all away in one trolley. Nor is having a little local monopoly on a fringe housing estate much good. More and more families have cars and do their shopping in a shopping centre. The crumbs that fall from the big high street stores are rarely able to support the small local shops nowadays.

What remains for the small retail trader? Well, special knowledge and skill, for a start. The classic example is the dispensing chemist: his trade is still to a great extent in private hands. But to become a qualified dispensing chemist requires years of training. Selling high class jewellery, specialised photographic equipment and the like successfully also requires a high degree of knowledge. And a considerable investment of both time and money is needed to establish a reputation and to acquire a sufficiently wide stockholding.

If there is a little 'making' as well as 'selling' in your shop, this can provide the necessary edge. Bakers bake as well as sell their bread and cakes. Butchers cut up their meat as well as hand it out over the counter. To make and sell is often a better bet, if the market is there and your product is really superior, than just to resell other firms' merchandise.

Sometimes it is possible to find a 'niche'. There may be a

demand for some class of goods not being supplied by the high street shops. If you are sure that the market is big enough and that you can capture it, this is almost certainly the best edge you can get. But you will need to do a great deal of market research and remain ever vigilant to ensure that you remain ahead of anyone who attempts to compete.

In my next example the entrepreneur is banking on:

- his know-how concerning a special range of goods
- having found a niche in the market
- an ingenious idea for helping to keep some major customers 'loyal'.

Example 4

Ourtown Electrical Supplies Ltd is acquiring the shop hitherto run by Joe Lamplight in Dogberry Street, Ourtown. Additional capital of £40,000 is needed to extend the services it offers to the electrical contractors in the borough.

History of the existing business
Joe Lamplight's father opened a shop selling electrical goods in High Street, Ourtown in 1933. He retired in 1962, when the High Street property was acquired by Pachyderm Developments plc under a compulsory purchase order of the then Ourtown Metropolitan Borough Council.

In order to carry on the business, Joe Lamplight took a lease on premises in Dogberry Street. This lease is about to expire and Joe, having reached retirement age, has offered the goodwill and stock of the business for sale.

The trade in large items of electrical household equipment such as cookers and TV sets has declined over the years, but the shop has maintained a steady turnover in the smaller items, especially lamps and light fittings. Sales to the public account for about half the turnover, sales at trade discount terms to local electricians and electrical contractors for the remainder.

In 1986 the turnover amounted to £79,000 and the gross profit to £19,250. The current stock is valued at £17,000, and Mr Lamplight is asking an additional £4,000 in consideration of his existing connections.

It is not intended to renew the lease at Dogberry Street. The company has obtained an option on the ground floor of the Ourtown Cooperative Society's former emporium in Verges Street. Although this is some distance from the main shopping centre, it is deemed suitable for the purposes of the company. A lease for 20 years is available at an initial annual rent of £10,250.

The market
Our initial marketing thrust will be directed to supplying the electrical contractors in Ourtown and surrounding districts. We shall maintain the existing retail trade and, indeed, increase our range.

Our long-term policy will be to establish a comprehensive retail trade in both electrical and electronic goods.

There are 29 electrical contractors in Ourtown and 20 more in the catchment area which includes Witherspool. The value of goods bought by those individuals and firms we have canvassed greatly exceeds half a million pounds a year. Many of these purchases will be made directly from the manufacturers, but at least two-thirds are obtained through wholsale suppliers in Bradfield, 20 miles distant over congested roads.

Lamplights have been attempting to meet this demand and are well thought of, but shortage of both money for stock and space to store and display it have limited the opportunities.

A canvass has been made of 30 of the potential customers, and this has produced a very encouraging response. There have been complaints, sometimes very bitter, about the infrequency and unreliability of the Bradfield suppliers' out-of-town deliveries, and a local supplier with a comprehensive stock would be very welcome.

Ten of the contractors have gone so far as to agree to invest in the new company, and Messrs Belt & Braces, Chartered Accountants, have suggested that use could be made of Business Expansion Scheme rules, enabling investment to be made by these contractors out of taxable income. This has been approved by the investors' own accountants.

The directors
There are three directors of Ourtown Electrical Supplies Ltd:

Robert Herrick, aged 30, will be managing director, with direct responsibility both for trade sales and running the shop. He has been, for the last five years, the manager of the Bradfield branch of Electron Suppliers Ltd, running almost exactly the same type of business. He had increased the turnover and profit for Electron every year by a greater margin than was shown by any other branch but had left because he saw no possibility for further promotion. Robert is married with one child. He is a BSc of London University and has attended management courses at Bradfield University's Department of Business Studies.

Joseph Lamplight, aged 64, the present proprietor of the business, has agreed to stay on as a part-time director for at least one year. He will attend the business as and when required. His experience of Ourtown conditions – he is a Rotarian and a member of the Chamber of Commerce – will be extremely valuable, as will his friendly relations with many of the customers. He will give all the help he can in the setting up of the new organisation.

Deidre Williams, aged 45, a graduate of Bradfield University, was, before her marriage, secretary to the regional chairman of the Home Counties Bank. Three years ago she returned to commerce as personal assistant to a director of Pachyderm Developments plc. She finds, however, that opportunities in this job are limited and has joined Robert Herrick to run this company. She will be in charge of administration and all financial aspects of the company.

Robert Herrick will provide £20,000 capital; Deidre Williams £10,000. Each will receive a salary of £12,000 per annum. Joseph Lamplight will receive £2,000 a year for his services and advice, payable quarterly.

Accountants are Messrs Belt & Braces.

Solicitors are Messrs Redd, Herring and Co of Dover Court, Ourtown.

Methods
On 30 November it is intended to move the whole of the existing stock to the new premises. These will have been refitted as a showroom, where members of the public as well as the trade purchasers can examine and select from the stock. There are extensive stock rooms at the rear and limited parking facilities by a side entrance where trade customers can pick up goods. The company's suppliers and own van driver can also use this entrance.

The company will offer the trade customers 25 per cent off list price, with additional discounts of 2½ per cent for payment within 30 days and 7½ per cent for cash on delivery. Delivery will be free within 10 miles for orders of more than £100, but a charge of £5 will be made for smaller orders. The company intends to make deliveries within eight hours inside this 10-mile radius.

The managing director plans to visit all trade clients and potential trade clients at least once every two months.

A brochure and a price-list of the company's main lines and items has been designed and is being printed.

On 7 December the company intends to open at the new premises with a formal gala to which all potential trade customers will be invited, together with the local press. Bobby Lovebird, the actress, who is, of course, a local girl, has kindly consented to be present for the formal opening ceremony.

One of the company's major concerns will be the proper control of purchasing and stock levels, and with this aim in view, it has engaged the services of Hepplewhite and Co to design a computerised stock control system. The directors believe that at £15,000 this system should pay for itself within a very short period.

Longer-term strategy

The directors have mapped out a five-year plan. In the earlier phases, the company will concentrate on the type of trade outlined above. However, sales to the public will not be neglected, and when the time is ripe, both financially and as indicated by a market survey, a major project for the sale of larger electrical items, such as cookers, washing machines, etc will be launched. This will probably necessitate raising more capital.

In five years BES investors in the company will be in a position to receive the rewards of their investment. It is hoped they will continue as shareholders, but in any case the company expects to be able to offer reasonable terms to buy them out, probably by means of a new share issue.

This is a company looking to expand, not only in the short term, but also to become a major trading organisation.

Financial requirements

The capital already subscribed or agreed to be subscribed is as follows:

	£	
Robert Herrick	20,000	
Deidre Williams	10,000	
Joseph Lamplight	4,000	(in satisfaction of the goodwill of his business)
Trade (BES) subscribers	20,000	
Total	£54,000	

The directors are asking for a development loan of £30,000 and an overdraft facility, to take care of temporary cash shortfalls, of £10,000.

The initial expenditure will be as follows:

	£
Payment to Joe Lamplight for stock	17,000
Additional starting stock	12,000
Fittings and alterations to new premises and van	12,500
Computer and software	20,000
Advertising and publicity	5,000
Six months' rent in advance	5,000
Sundries	2,000
Total	£73,500

The balance of £6,500, together with the overdraft facility, should provide sufficient working capital, as will be seen from the enclosed cash flow forecast.

Financial forecasts
On the basis of forecasts of sales and costs, Messrs Belt & Braces have produced the enclosed statements of anticipated overheads, profits and cash flow.

As will be seen, the directors are budgeting for a profit of £9,000, a bank balance of £14,000, and reduction of the term loan by repayment of £18,000.

If the budgeted figures are fulfilled, the balance sheets at the end of the year should show the following:

Assets	£	£
Goodwill		4,000
Fittings and equipment	32,500	
less Depreciation	8,125	24,375
Stock in trade		29,000
Debtors	35,145	
less Creditors	26,218	
VAT owing	5,458	3,469
Cash		14,218
		£75,062
Represented by		
Loan	30,000	
less Refund	18,000	12,000
Share capital	54,000	
Profit and Loss account	9,062	
Shareholders' funds		63,062
		£75,062

The directors do not propose to pay a dividend for at least the first year but will use the anticipated cash surplus to develop the retail side of the business, ie the sale of refrigerators, cookers, TV sets, etc.

In the second year, if all goes well, it is hoped to achieve a turnover of £500,000, with a net profit of £35,000.

Ourtown Electrical Supplies Ltd

Financial projections for first year of trading

Overhead Schedule

	Month 12	Month 1	Month 2	Month 3	Month 4	Month 5	Month 6	Month 7	Month 8	Month 9	Month 10	Month 11	Carry Forward	Total
Rent	5126						2563			2563				10251
Rates	305	305	305	305	305	305	305	305	305	305				3050
Directors' fees	1667	1667	2166	1667	1667	2166	1667	1667	2166	1667	1667	2166		21997
Electricity				700			600			550			700	2550
Gas				200			150			100			175	625
Insurance (inc motor)	875													875
Bank charges			75			75			75			75		300
Licence fees (inc motor)	100													100
Wages	1800	1800	1800	1800	1800	1800	1800	1800	1800	1800	1800	1800		21600
PAYE and NICs				378			378			378			378	1512
Total non-VATable	9873	3772	4346	5050	3772	4346	7463	3772	4346	7363	3467	4041	1253	62864
Advertising	5000	150	150	150	150	150	150	150	150	150	150	150		6650
Petrol and oil	120	120	120	120	120	120	120	120	120	120	120	120		1440
Motor repairs			100			100			100			100		400
Telephone	200			175			175			175			175	900
Sundries	100	100	100	100	100	100	100	100	100	100	100	100		1200
Professional fees	750			200			200			200			400	1750
														0
														0
Total VATable	6170	370	470	745	370	470	745	370	470	745	370	470	575	12340
VAT	926	56	71	112	56	71	112	56	71	112	56	71	86	1851
Total Overheads	16969	4198	4887	5907	4198	4887	8320	4198	4887	8220	3893	4582	1914	77055

Illustration 8

71

Profit and Loss Account

	Month 12	Month 1	Month 2	Month 3	Month 4	Month 5	Month 6	Month 7	Month 8	Month 9	Month 10	Month 11	Total
Sales	27500	21500	23250	26600	29600	29600	29600	29600	22200	34000	37000	37000	347450
less													0
Cost of goods sold	18163	15875	16838	19355	21680	21680	21680	21680	16260	24775	27100	27100	252186
Overheads	6267	6267	6267	6267	6267	6267	6267	6267	6267	6267	6267	6267	75204
Interest on overdraft	0	0	25	18	0	0	0	0	0	0	0	0	43
Interest on loan	333	315	298	280	263	245	228	210	193	175	158	140	2838
Depreciation	677	677	677	677	677	677	677	677	677	677	677	677	8124
Net profit	2060	-1634	-855	3	713	731	748	766	-1197	2106	2798	2816	9055

Cash flow forecast

	Month 12	Month 1	Month 2	Month 3	Month 4	Month 5	Month 6	Month 7	Month 8	Month 9	Month 10	Month 11
Sales-payments	7906	25156	26263	27399	30875	33523	34040	34040	31913	30199	37927	42033
Loans	30000											
Capital introduced	50000											
Total receipts	87906	25156	26263	27399	30875	33523	34040	34040	31913	30199	37927	42033
Purchases payments	3469	33044	18367	19653	22526	24932	24932	24932	24309	19678	28759	31165
Overheads	16968	4197	4887	5906	4197	4887	8319	4197	4887	8219	3892	4582
Interest			970			806			630			473
Drawings												
Loan repayments	1500	1500	1500	1500	1500	1500	1500	1500	1500	1500	1500	1500
Capital items	37375	0	0	0	0	0	0	0	0	0	0	0
Opening stock	17000	0	0	0	0	0	0	0	0	0	0	0
VAT	0	0	0	-5347	0	0	2982	0	0	3265	0	0
Total payments	76312	38741	25724	21712	28223	32125	37733	30629	31326	32662	34151	37720
Cash flow	11594	-13585	539	5687	2652	1398	-3693	3411	587	-2463	3776	4313
Bank												
Opening balance	0	11594	-1991	-1452	4235	6887	8285	4592	8003	8590	6127	9903
Closing balance	11594	-1991	-1452	4235	6887	8285	4592	8003	8590	6127	9903	14216

Illustration 9

Chapter 5
Manufacturing

For an inventor the path is hard and steep. The continuing progress of the human race depends on him, and yet often he is the last to benefit from his own ingenuity. Although, of course, not all inventions or ideas are practical, a fair proportion will turn out to be commercially viable. But to get them into production and sold – there's the rub!

If you are an inventor, your first priority must be to protect your invention. By all means, see a patent agent and get it registered. That is essential. But patents give very limited protection, and the registration procedure is cumbersome and expensive. Your best policy is to get production going and saturate the market fast. Once you have succeeded in that, your patent has acquired value.

As an inventor, you are faced with a choice of two basic strategies: you can adopt the 'paddle your own canoe' line, or you can sell your invention to a large concern, for a lump sum or for royalties. Either way, there are problems, and your first planning decision must be to choose between the two courses. Two examples are given in this chapter to illustrate these alternatives.

An example of someone who possesses skills neither in design nor marketing but does have the ability to organise a production unit and can afford what is, in effect, a service to other manufacturers, is also shown.

Example 5

This is a request for further capital to produce and test prototypes for a new automatic car seat-belt reel. A sum of £4,000 is needed.

1. There have been continual complaints about the inconvenience of the seat-belt reels now on the market for two-door saloon cars. Much annoyance is caused to passengers entering the rear and entangling themselves in the slack of the front-seat safety belts. The problem has been to reconcile the need for a firm, reliable re-wind with the safety requirements of an inertia mechanism

75

which will hold the belt tight when the car stops suddenly. I enclose several cuttings from motoring magazines commenting on this. I have been assured that a better type of reel would have great popular appeal, and I think I have solved the problem.

2. My name is Marcus Garside. I am a trained mechanical engineer at present employed in the Quality Control Department of Brytelook Engineering Ltd in Witherspool. In the last three years I have spent my spare time designing and making the first prototype of my new reel.

3. I enclose drawings of the design which has been tested for efficiency and reliability in three different models of car. EC patents have been obtained through Messrs Seek and Find, patent agents of Bradfield, and a US patent has been applied for. I have spent £3,500 in cash of my own money on this project to date.

4. The design is capable of improvement, now the principle has been shown to work. The design may also have to be modified for production. For both these reasons I wish to employ the services of a design engineering consultancy. The cost could well amount to £3,000, but I hope to obtain a grant of 50 per cent of this under the new government Innovation Initiative Scheme. Subsequently I would want to produce a run of six prototypes, both for testing and for submission to potential buyers of my patent, the testing to be done at the Bridgeworth Engineering College or at the British Institute for Automobile Engineering.

The money would be spent as follows:

	£
Consultancy (net)	1,500
Prototypes	1,000
Testing	2,000
Sundries and expenses	2,000

I am able to put a further £2,500 of my own money into the project, and I am asking the Deeside County Council Enterprise Fund to lend me the additional £4,000 needed.

5. I do not intend to produce or sell this product myself. I have neither the resources nor the temperament to run a production unit of my own. It will be my object to sell the design and patent rights to a firm capable of exploiting it to the full. There are two firms in the county capable of producing the belt reel.

Next, let us consider a team which has a patent and, believing its product to be a commercial proposition, wishes to produce and market it as well. The combination of two men, both in the same line of business, one with marketing, the other with production skills, will obviously be stronger than either alone, and they have been wise enough to invite a colleague to join them, albeit part-time, a man with the financial knowledge and skills to keep them in line over their cash problems.

They have also agreed that their main aim in the first year will be to set up an efficient production system.

Although the managing director will pay a great deal of attention to the marketing of their products, they have decided to defer setting up their own selling organisation for the time being and rely on sales through another firm. Time will tell whether the strategy will pay off, but at least it gives a management limited in number a chance to succeed.

Example 6

This is a project to manufacture left-handed snooker cues for which we have identified an expanding market. We need additional finance of £50,000.

Our market
The Snooker Cue Maker Society's annual report for 1985 gives the total number of cues sold in the period September 1984 – August 1985 as XX thousand. All the major cue makers make only right-handed cues.

Published figures (HMSO Statistics of Handedness, 1983) show that 7.8 per cent of males aged between 10 and 60 are left-handed to the extent that they have difficulty in using right-handed tools.

A sample survey of 452 interviews with left-handed men showed that:

72% did not want to play snooker
10% would play if left-handed cues were available
7% played with right-handed cues without difficulty
9% played with right-handed cues with great difficulty
2% refused to answer

From the above figures we have deduced that there is a potential market for between 50,000 and 80,000 left-handed cues per annum.

We interviewed Hector McWhirter, the 1985 St Kilda and Rockall Snooker Champion, who is known to be left-handed. Mr McWhirter uses a custom-made left-handed cue. He told us that until he had such a cue specially made, he was 'getting nowhere'. He said that the new cue had added 25 points per frame to his game. Mr McWhirter has offered to sponsor our venture but would expect a small fee.

Fifty-five per cent of snooker cues are distributed through three main agents and 45 per cent directly through the normal retail channels. We have decided, in view of our limited sales and distribution facilities, to sell through the leading agents. Galligaskin and Breeks Ltd have agreed to place an initial order of 1,000 and to join with us in a sales and publicity campaign.

The directors
James Turbotte, aged 37, is the founder of the company. Since leaving school all his career has been spent in the sports goods industry:

1965–68 Trainee at Consolidated Cricket Bats Ltd
1968–73 Salesman for Hurry & Push Ltd in their Sports Goods Department
1973–78 Assistant Sales Manager, Potpink Ltd
1978–85 Sales Manager, Potpink Ltd

In 1984 Potpink Ltd was taken over by Sportsell Inc, and in December 1985 Turbotte was made redundant. Since then, in conjuction with Brian Fletcher, he has been developing the new left-handed cue and doing the necessary market research. He thinks he can claim that nobody knows the snooker cue market better than he does. He has invested his savings of £10,500 in the company and has taken out a second mortgage on his house to raise a further £24,000.

Brian Fletcher, aged 29, holds the City and Guilds Certificate (Grade 4) in snooker cue making. He has spent all his working life in the Cue Department of Potpink Ltd. For three years he was manager in charge of technical developments. He, too, was made redundant when Sportsell transferred production to Korea in 1986. He has helped to design the new cue and will be production director. By remortgaging his house, he has raised £10,500 to invest in the company.

Julian Watchman, aged 25, is a chartered accountant. He is employed by a local firm of accountants but has been given permission by them to serve on the company's board as financial director. He has borrowed £12,500 from family sources to invest in the company.

Auditors: Messrs Belt & Braces, Queen Street, Ourtown
Solicitors: Messrs Manyana, Manyana & Holliday

The product
Our cue has been designed for left-handed players by realigning the grip at the butt end, by adjusting the torque in the shaft, and by using a special tip invented by Brian Fletcher (EC Patent No 158692). This allows a left-handed player the same freedom of arm action as his right-handed rival. Independent tests, see below, have shown that:

Grip realignment alone has improved accuracy in the cue ball by 7.13 per cent and the accuracy of path of the object ball by 6.78 per cent.

Torque adjustment alone has improved accuracy in the cue ball by 2.38 per cent and path accuracy of the object ball by 2.86 per cent.

The new tip (the Accutip) alone improved cue ball accuracy by 11.29 per cent and object ball accuracy by 13.17 per cent.

The overall improvement in accuracy, using all three together, was cue ball, 18.72 per cent; object ball, 19.98 per cent.

Technical experts tell us that 'counter-compensation' accounts for the total improvement being less than the sum of the individual gains.

We intend to take advantage of the skill and experience of Brian Fletcher to manufacture the cues ourselves, save that we propose to sub-contract out the final lacquering and painting.

We have selected the necessary machinery, and the special tools have been designed. By using good second-hand equipment, we should not have to spend more than £46,000 in all on machinery and tools.

Costings based on quotations received, and the best possible estimates at the time of going to press, indicate an ex-works cost per cue of approximately £16. Galligaskin and Breeks, on their initial order, have contracted to pay £30 per cue, leaving £14 to cover overheads and profit. (See financial forecasts appended.)

Our cues, therefore, should sell in the shops at a price of £70 each. This is about 8 per cent more than the price of a 'Championship' standard right-handed cue, but we believe that the increased efficiency of our product for left-handers will more than compensate for this and allow us to prosper in the market.

The Snooker Players Association was good enough to arrange for independent testing of the cue. The results, summarised above, are set out in Appendix 2.

Our short-term strategy

With our limited resources of both workforce and money, we cannot have, at this stage, a marketing policy that involves our own sales force and distributional system. For that reason we have entered into a contract, for one year, with Galligaskin and Breeks Ltd of London, under which they will market our product on an exclusive basis. They have undertaken to place an initial contract for not less than 5,000 cues. Galligaskin and Breeks have agreed to meet 50 per cent of advertising and publicity costs for the launch up to an agreed sum.

We have planned a publicity and advertising campaign with emphasis on a presence at all major tournaments during the next year in the UK.

James Turbotte will be responsible for all marketing and also the overall day-to-day control.

Brian Fletcher will manage all production, purchasing and transport. He will be aided by an assistant manager who will have special responsibility for quality control.

Julian Watchman will be a non-executive director but will attend the weekly management meetings we intend to hold and will oversee the finances of the company. An office manager has been appointed.

Suitable premises have been acquired on a seven-year lease in the old Copperbottom Mill, Ourtown. We move in on 1 October.

Second-hand machinery of excellent quality is obtainable, save that we shall have to have a special tool to our own design made by Dropforge and Lathe of Milston. Designs for this tool have been agreed. Delivery is promised by 1 October.

Very favourable terms have been quoted for the final lacquering and painting, which is being sub-contracted out, by at least two firms of repute.

Four skilled cue-makers have been recruited and, with five unskilled persons, should suffice for production of up to 350 cues per week. We envisage a total workforce of 14 persons other than the directors. Each additional quantity of 100 cues per week will mean an increase in staff, which we will meet through a training programme. We believe that the machinery and equipment which we have or propose to buy will cover production needs of up to 750 cues per week. The premises are adequate for up to 1,000 cues per week.

Our office manager is an experienced bookkeeper. We intend to run a full set of weekly management accounts, together with a daily update, for the managing director, of cash, debtors, orders on hand, etc. Our books will be kept manually for the time being, but a small personal computer is available for the customer database and other management uses.

Our long-term strategy

The sports goods market is highly competitive, especially for games that are as popular and widely played as snooker. Our patents will give us some protection, but we believe that our long-term success will depend on our building up a very high share of the market.

Our five-year strategy, therefore, will be as follows:

1. To build up, in the first year, an expandable production capacity
2. To build in, at the same time, reliable systems of quality control. We are engaging Krishnan-Davis Associates as consultants in this field and are

applying for a Department of Trade and Industry grant to enable us to pay their fees

3. To investigate the market opportunities both in the UK and overseas
4. In the second and subsequent years, to create our own company sales and marketing division to exploit any additional markets
5. To develop the Accutip for use in standard right-handed cues. Whether we shall extend our manufacturing to include making right-handed cues ourselves, or whether we shall license the Accutip to other manufacturers, will depend on the market conditions and resources available at the time
6. To keep our eyes open for the acquisition of any company whose business would support or enhance the production or sale of our product. We should, however, not allow the purchase of such a company to divert resources from our main objective.

We fully intend to be a major force in our own market within a five-year period. The rapid expansion envisaged makes it unlikely that any cash will be available for the payment of dividends within the five-year period.

Financial requirements
We are seeking a loan, under the Loan Guarantee Scheme, of £50,000.

Additional capital of £40,000 is being subscribed by the directors to make a total ordinary share capital of £57,000 as follows:

	£
James Turbotte	34,500
Brian Fletcher	10,500
Julian Watchman	12,500
	£57,500

The additional capital will be used as follows:

	£
Plant and machinery	46,000
Office equipment	6,000
Personal computer and software	5,000
Sundry start-up costs	2,000
Working capital	31,000
	£90,000

Two motor cars and a van are being acquired under a leasing arrangement.

Financial expectations
We are enclosing, as Appendix 4, a financial business model drawn up for us by Messrs Belt & Braces.

We have a sales target of 16,500 cues for the first 12 months. Based on this, our profit and loss account for the year will be as follows:

	£	£
Sales		500,000
less Establishment costs (rent, fuel, etc)	60,000	
Directors' fees	41,000	
Office and administration	27,000	
Professional fees	15,000	
Advertising and publicity	30,000	
Sundries and contingency	10,000	
Interest payable	5,000	
Depreciation	17,500	
	205,500	
Wages and materials	270,000	
Subcontracting	50,000	525,000
Net loss for year		£25,500

The intention is to double sales and production in the second year. With a turnover of £1 million per annum (33,500 cues), our profit and loss account should be as follows:

	£	£
Sales		1,000,000
less Establishment costs	62,500	
Directors' fees	41,000	
Office and administration	30,000	
Professional fees	10,000	
Advertising and publicity	45,000	
Sundries and contingency	10,000	
Interest payable	2,000	
Depreciation	17,500	
	218,000	
Wages and materials	540,000	
Subcontracting	100,000	858,000
Net profit for year		£142,000

Under their service contracts, the two working directors, James Turbotte and Brian Fletcher, are entitled to a bonus of 5 per cent on all net profit over £20,000. Their bonus for the second year, on the above forecast, would be £6,100 each.

We are enclosing the following appendices:

1. Market survey figures of left-handed snooker players
2. Test results from the Snooker Players Association
3. Copy of agreement for one year with Galligaskin and Breeks Ltd
4. Financial forecasts produced by Messrs Belt & Braces
5. Service contracts for each director.

Example 7

I am Rita Fairhurst of 11 Thompson Street, Ourtown OU3 7JK. I wish to borrow £5,000 to start a business, making up garments for designers of ladies' fashions producing relatively small collections.

My market
There are more than 18 ladies' fashion designers within easy travelling distance of Ourtown. They design, and sell through their own outlets and specialist retailers, a wide range of dresses, blouses, skirts, etc. Their field is the middle range, between the expensive designer 'labels' and the mass-produced lines sold in chain stores. In my present job I have come into contact with most of these designers, and I have consulted all but three about my project.

Of the designers visited:

- six both cut and make up their own garments
- three cut their own garments but have them made up by outmakers
- three cut their own garments and use outmakers to some extent
- three have all their garments both cut and made up by outmakers.

The nine who use outmakers are my natural target. I estimate their probable weekly production and sales as follows:

- one produces and sells 300 or more garments per week
- two produce and sell between 250 and 300 garments per week
- three produce and sell between 150 and 250 garments per week
- three produce and sell less than 150 garments per week.

I estimate the total production of these nine firms to average 1,800 garments per week. Twenty per cent of these are probably beyond my scope, but that leaves over 1,400. This is without counting the possibility of getting work from firms which at present make up their own garments but may need extra capacity. The heads of many of these firms have told me of difficulties in running their own making-up rooms and have indicated that they will give me trial orders as soon as I set up in business.

My background
I am 34 years of age and have spent all my life in the industry since leaving school at 18. Realising that I had no talent for design, I have concentrated on the cutting and making up. For the last nine years I have been supervisor for Dodson and Fogg Ltd, in charge of 16 girls. As Dodson and Fogg have been taken over and production is being moved to Glasgow, I have become redundant.

I have my savings and redundancy pay, together amounting to £6,500, and can offer a second mortgage on my house as security for a loan.

What I propose to do
There are 2,000 sq ft of workshop space available in the old Merchant Mill at Witherspool. The rent is £2,750 and the rates are £845. I estimate it will cost £2,000 for renovation.

Four of the girls who have worked with me at Dodson's would be happy to work for me in my new venture. They are all first class workers. I believe I would have less difficulty than most in recruiting extra staff. I have a friend, Joy Kerner, at present chief bookkeeper at Wormoulds. She would join me and be responsible for all office work and correspondence.

I propose initially to concentrate on making-through. Each girl will be paid on a time basis, with bonuses for production and quality.

As supervisor I have been involved in setting prices and therefore have a very good idea of the labour costs for different styles and garments. As the garments will be supplied cut and trimmed, there are few direct costs in terms of materials, threads, zips, linings, etc.

I expect to start with the equivalent of eight girls working a five-hour day each. The actual hours each girl works will depend on her availability, most of the girls being mothers with children.

The machines I shall need and plan to lease are as follows:

2 × 5-thread safety stitch	£18 a week
6 × lockstitch	£42 a week
1 × buttonstitcher and buttonholer	£45 a week

I know where I can obtain second-hand refurbished machines of good quality on a leasing arrangement. The total weekly cost to me should be approximately £105. I estimate that, in addition, maintenance will average £35 per week.

In the longer term
My longer-term strategy will be:

- to expand the making up business as outlined above
- to develop the work to include cutting and trimming, which could be more profitable
- to own my own machines
- to expand into longer run production
- to maintain a high level of quality control.

I intend, as far as possible, to finance all expansion out of retained profits.

Appendices
I enclose herewith:

1. Schedule of nine local designers who use outmakers, together with my estimates of the average weekly number of garments to be made up
2. Cash flow forecast for 12 months, beginning April, based on an average price to be charged of £9 per garment plus VAT.

The steps that Rita takes to produce the cash flow forecast (Illustration 10) are based on the procedures laid down in Chapter 2. Rita is using the National Westminster Bank's cash flow form, but she has the new 12-month form, unlike Alexander Battersby (Example 1), who used the older six-month form.

A. Rita writes in all the certain fixed overheads, including VAT where applicable:
   1. *Rent* — £2,750 per annum = £687.50 per quarter, no VAT, payable quarterly in advance.
   2. *Rates* — £848 per annum, no VAT, payable in 10 monthly instalments, beginning April.
   3. *Costs for leasing equipment* — £105 per week net = £483 per four-week period, including VAT. The terms of the lease

stipulate 12 weeks' rent in advance, ie £1,449 including VAT, the first payment to be made for July at the end of June.

Note. This arrangement takes care of the fact that there are 13 four-week periods in a calendar year.

4. *Regular wages* — The only full-time employee will be Joy Kerner. The eight part-time machinists will work irregular hours; but for the purpose of the cash flow forecast, Rita will assume that their weekly hours are 8 × 25 = 200, which, at £4 per hour, works out at £800 per week. Adding in Joy's wage of £600 per month brings the monthly wage bill to £4,065 per month. However, not all of this is payable immediately. There will be deductions of PAYE and NIC. These will vary from person to person, so Rita makes an estimate of 10 per cent, ie £406, adds on the employer's NIC, and arrives at a quarterly payment for PAYE and NIC of £1,800. Since no doubt the employees will be taking time off during the holiday months of July and August without benefit of holiday pay, the wages bill for these months is reduced by 30 per cent.

5. *Drawings* — Rita realises that to get her venture off the ground she will have to scrimp and scrape personally and take as little money as possible out of the business. She thinks she will just about get by on drawings of £375 per month.

6. *Loan repayments* — Because, as pointed out in Chapter 8, working capital requirements for this type of business are high, Rita is asking the bank for a repayment 'holiday' of 12 months. Therefore, no repayments are entered in this cash flow.

7. *Interest* — This is payable, however.

8. *Maintenance* — Payable on the hired equipment @ £35 per week net, ie £174 per month including VAT.

B. Next, Rita tackles overheads that are less certain in amount:

1. *Heating and lighting* — Estimated at £300 per quarter in arrears, no VAT payable.

2. *Insurances* — £250 in the first month, £325 in December for renewal of car insurance and licence, no VAT payable.

3. *Telephone* — £100 installation fee in first month; £115 per quarter in arrears including VAT.

4. *Petrol* etc — £56 per month including VAT.

5. *Stationery and printing* — £160 in first month, including

VAT; £20 per month, including VAT, thereafter.

6. *Sundries* — £20 per month including VAT.

7. *Repairs and contingencies* — Rita will allow £50 per month including VAT.

Note. Some of these items Rita had to add together in order to include them on the bank's form, as will be seen in Illustration 10.

C. Rita now writes in the start-up payments and receipts, as follows:

1. *Capital items* — £2,000 to refit the premises, plus £1,000 for office fixtures, etc, making a total of £3,450 including VAT.

2. *Loan received* — as applied for, £5,000, plus capital introduced, £6,500, totalling £11,500.

D. Rita believes she has canvassed enough potential customers to produce orders for the first month of 700 garments. She believes this will prove to be the average monthly output during her first year, save for the holiday months of July and August, when she expects her output to drop to 350 garments per month. She hopes to be sending out invoices for 700 × £9 = £6,300 worth of goods which, with VAT, will total £7,245, except for July and August, when the turnover, inclusive of VAT, is expected to be £3,622. As Rita will be paid one month in arrears, the first £7,245 will appear in the 'Sales-Debtors' line in May, and the two bad months for receipts will be August and September.

E. VAT must now be calculated. This will be payable in July, October and January. The July payment will be calculated from the VAT on the sales receipts for May and June (£14,490 × 15/115 = £1,890), less the VATable expenses for April, May and June. These latter include the capital items, the petrol, lease payments, telephone, maintenance costs and the sundries. For the three months these total £6,717, and the VAT included in this figure is £6,617 × 15/115 = £863. The VAT Rita will have to account for and pay in July is £1,890 − £863 = £1,027. By similar calculation the amount due in October is £1,520, and in January £2,565.

F. Next, the interest will be calculated. As the bank balance should be always in the black, the only interest payable will be

Rita Fairhurst

Enter Month	April		May		June		July		August	
Figures rounded to £'s	Budget	Actual	Budget	Actual	Budget	Actual	Budget	Actual	Budget	Actual
Receipts 1 Sales (inc VAT)-Cash			7,245		7,245		7,245		3,622	
2 -Debtors										
3 Other Trading Income										
4 Loans Received	5,000									
5 Capital Introduced	6,500									
6 Disposal of Assets										
7 Other Receipts										
A Total Receipts	11,500		7,245		7,245		7,245		3,622	
Payments 8 Cash Purchases										
9 Payments to Creditors										
10 Principal's Remuneration	375		375		375		375		375	
11 Wages/Salaries (net)	3,659		3,659		3,659		2,650		2,650	
12 PAYE/NI					1,800					
13 Capital Items	3,450									
14 Petrol etc	56		56		56		56		56	
15 Rent/Rates	772		85		85		772		85	
16 Services							300			
17 Leasing	1,449				483		483		483	
18 Maintenance	174		174		174		174		174	
19 Interest					163					
20 Bank/Finance Charges										
21 Professional Fees										
22 Telephone	115						126			
23 Insurance	250									
24 Printing, Sundries	250		90		90		90		90	
25										
26 VAT							1,027			
27 Corporation Tax etc										
28 Dividends										
B Total Payments	10,550		4,439		6,885		6,053		3,913	
C Net Cashflow (A − B)	950		2,806		360		1,192		−291	
29 Opening Bank Balance	0		950		3,756		4,116		5,308	
D Closing Bank Balance (C ± Line 29)	950		3,756		4,116		5,308		5,017	

Basic Assumptions – Please specify the following assumptions used in completing this form and list any other relevant ones overleaf:
– Credit Taken — the average period taken from creditors. _____ Days
– Credit Given — the average period given to debtors. __30__ Days

September		October		November		December		January		February		March		Total	
Budget	Actual	Budget	Actual	Budget	Actual	Budget	Actual	Budget	Actual	Budget	Actual	Budget	Actual	Budget	Actual
3,622		7,245		7,245		7,245		7,245		7,245		7,245		72,449	
														5,000	
														6,500	
3,622		7,245		7,245		7,245		7,245		7,245		7,245		83,949	
375		375		375		375		375		375		375		4,500	
3,659		3,659		3,659		3,659		3,659		3,659		3,659		41,890	
1,300						1,800						1,800		6,700	
														3,450	
56		56		56		56		56		56		56		672	
85		772		85		85		772						3,598	
		300						300						900	
483		483		483		483		483		483		483		6,279	
174		174		174		174		174		174		174		2,088	
162						163						162		650	
		126						126						493	
						325								575	
90		90		90		90		90		90		90		1,240	
		1,520						2,565						5,112	
6,385		7,555		4,922		7,210		8,600		4,837		6,800		78,147	
−2,763		−310		2,323		36		−1,355		2,408		446			
5,017		2,254		1,944		4,267		4,303		2,948		5,356			
2,254		1,944		4,267		4,303		2,948		5,356		5,802			

Illustration 10

on the term loan of £4,500. At 13 per cent, this works out at £146.25 per quarter.

G. Finally, the columns and rows are added up and the monthly bank balances determined.

Chapter 6
Expanding a Business

One need hardly point out that it is easier to obtain funds to expand an existing business than to get money to start one from scratch, that is, assuming the business has been reasonably successful. Raising money to rescue an ailing business is at least as difficult as obtaining it for a start-up. This chapter deals with the expansion of businesses with a fair track record.

There are three good, obvious reasons why money for expansion is easier to come by than finance for a brand new business:

1. The fact that there is a market for your product or service has already been demonstrated.
2. You and your team have shown yourselves capable of running a business, at least so far.
3. The business is already profitable.

One other advantage is that you know, from first-hand experience, what is going on in your business, what the problems are and what are the real possibilities. This will be apparent and inspire confidence, provided your plan for expansion is clearly presented.

In writing your plan, you will start, of course, with a brief history of your business, what it has done, what it is doing, the difficulties it has faced and overcome, and the problems and opportunities it now has to solve or exploit and for which the money is needed. A brief schedule of the turnover and profits of the last few years will refer to fuller accounts and balance sheets in your first appendix.

Although you have established that you have a satisfactory market, you still have to convince your reader that the market is big enough to absorb the products of your expansion or that the new markets you hope to penetrate will be receptive to your goods or services. As you will have been listening to your customers' feedback of comment and continuing your market research and exploration, this should not be too difficult.

The section on management is another matter. When you wrote your first or start-up business plan, you had to sell yourself as a manager, and personal details mattered. Now you have proved yourself, at least as far as running your business at its present size is concerned. However, on the assumption that you are requiring finance for a significant increase in output, your business will be seen as about to enter a new phase, in which the old patterns and methods of management may well have to change.

For example, up to now, if there was a production crisis, you could call for more overtime from the team, take off your jacket, sit down at the bench and solve the problems by your own efforts. If next week looked bad for orders, a few phone calls one morning might well work wonders. Or, if there was a shortfall of cash, you could draw out less for yourself for a week or two, postpone the odd payment or ring up a big debtor and cajole a payment out of him. As your business gets bigger, this style of 'crisis management' just will not work as it did.

As you will remember, it was argued in Chapter 5 that it takes an exceptional genius to maintain detailed control of a business above a certain level. It may be that you will not reach that level, even with the planned expansion. Perhaps the employment of a competent works foreman, the installation of a good management accounting system and the help, when needed, of the local Enterprise Agency or Small Firms Service will see you through. There is no need to elaborate a management system.

However, experience does show that when a substantial amount of new money is needed for expansion, the business will also need a change of management style and an infusion of supplementary management skills. Some venture capital firms even insist on introducing some of their own management skills, almost always financial control, into the business in which they are investing. The management system is very important, and it is worth spending time and effort to convince the readers of your plan that you recognise the problem and have a management strategy which is balanced and will work.

There are two other sections of your business plan which will require special attention when money is sought for expansion. In the Introduction, four ways of achieving success in a competitive world were suggested:

1. Innovation
2. Cheaper products
3. Better service
4. Better quality of goods.

Expansion means moving out into a world where you hope to be a bigger fish in a bigger pond. Your choice from the above alternative strategies becomes more crucial. When you write your plan you must make clear which strategy or strategies you are choosing and show that you understand the management consequences of your decision. For instance, if 'innovation' is your choice, in order to maintain progress the money you plough back into the business should go largely into research and development.

If you choose the 'cheaper product' line of action – which can be very dangerous for a small business – your policy must be to minimise overheads and to keep the marginal cost of production as low as possible.

'Better service' involves top managerial attention to matters such as delivery dates, after-sales visits to customers or clients, a financial policy with relatively high overheads and high profit margins.

'Better quality of goods' commits you to a high degree of design innovation and the strictest quality control. Make sure that the section of the business plan labelled 'Strategy' or 'The longer-term view' shows your tactics and management to be in harmony with the overall strategy.

You must also give special attention to that part of your plan which deals with the use to which you intend to put the money you are seeking.

First, *do* ask for a large enough sum, more even than you think you will need. You may have heard the story of the bank manager who, when asked for a loan of £30,000, automatically offered £20,000 (secured, of course); then, when his customer failed for lack of sufficient capital, congratulated himself on having prevented the man from losing £10,000 more! It is to be hoped that this type of bank manager is now extinct. However, you would be wise to make sure you are not under-capitalised. Ask for plenty. You may need it for a crisis you cannot foresee. If you are offered less, don't be afraid to turn it down!

The section on finance will be of special importance to your lender. It is here he will expect to find out what is in the deal for him. You may be able to raise the equity through the Business

Expansion Scheme. In this section you must explain, as fully as you can, how your backers will get their reward for entrusting their money to you for your business.

Two examples will serve to illustrate this chapter. The first is a very simple application for funds to carry out further work on a canal-side marina and involves neither marketing nor management problems; the second is an approach by an imaginary technological company trying to raise money for the manufacture of an imaginary product. The commercial aspects will be dealt with here.

In the case of the marina, a simple cash flow forecast, such as could be produced by the owner himself, is appended (Illustration 12). In the case of the high-tech manufacturer, the financial modelling and projections could be the responsibility of a specialist accountant. The problems of organisation are concentrated on and no attempt is made to give financial forecasts either of profit and loss or cash flow.

Example 8

The Wagbatch Marina Ltd is seeking a loan of £25,000 to finance the second stage of the marina project at Wagbatch on the Dove and Derwent Canal.

History
I, John S Brook, having some time ago inherited 20 acres of land immediately adjoining the Dove and Derwent Canal, was made redundant by the Megapolitan Engineering Company plc in 1985. I used £20,000 of my redundancy money to excavate and develop a 45-berth marina for canal boats, which was completed in the late summer of 1986. Such was the demand that the company was able to let 30 berths to overwintering craft, and the whole marina was full during the summer of 1987 and has continued to be so through the winter of 1987/88.

The company also runs a Calor gas supply service to the boat owners (and others), and in the summer opened a small shop to supply the passing trade.

As will be seen from the enclosed accounts (Appendix A), mooring fees amounted to £15,000 during the first year to 30 September 1987; gas sales to £1,087; and shop sales to £3,963. The profit, after payment of all expenses, amounted to £1,017.

The market
The use of the English canals and waterways for pleasure boating, whether by traditional style 7-foot wide longboats or by smaller cruisers, has been increasing by 5 per cent a year over the last few years and shows no sign of decreasing. More derelict canals are being brought back into use by the joint efforts of volunteer enthusiasts and the British Waterways Board. With increasing numbers of boats on the water, the demand for permanent berths in off-canal marinas exceeds the places available. The company had to turn away at least 20 applicants for berths during the course of the autumn of 1987.

There is also an increasing demand for other facilities, ie canal-side shopping for the summer boat users, and Calor gas, especially during the colder months, etc. The company has considered the provision of diesel fuel for the boats but, as yet, is not convinced of the profitability.

Sales and service

The company charges 60p plus VAT per foot-length of boat per month under six-monthly contracts.

Boats can vary in length from about 24 to 70 ft, with a mean length of 30 ft. This gives an annual rental per boat of £216 plus VAT.

The company has an arrangement with the British Waterways Board whereby the annual BWB licence fee is collected from the boat owners and paid over to the BWB, less a collecting discount of 5 per cent.

Other sources of income are the profits from the sale of Calor gas and from the shop sales.

A rental of £4,500 per annum is paid to the Waterways Board for the access to the canal itself.

What the company will do

During the summer of 1988 the company will excavate and line with concrete an extension to the existing marina. The work will be relatively easy because no additional access to the canal is required and because the level of the canal itself is 3 ft higher than the average height of the area to be excavated.

The company has a provisional contract with Reilly Contractors for the construction. They will supply earth-moving equipment, shuttering and labour, and Wagbatch will supply materials. Plans have been drawn up by C Wren and Associates, the architects, and approved by the local authority.

It is hoped that the work will be completed during September, in time for overwinter letting, beginning in October.

The extra rental fees to be obtained per year are estimated to be in the region of £10,000 plus VAT. As the extra annual costs involved in these rentals are very small, the increase in annual profit will be very close to this extra rental.

Long-term plans

The object of the enterprise is to provide me with a long-term income for my semi-retirement and for later years. There are plans to extend the marina to a total of 100 berths. Plans are also in hand for the leasing of part of the land for a boat repairing yard. The person who would run this yard is negotiating with CoSIRA for financial and other support. Eventually the shop is to be let, and possibly also the Calor gas sales business.

By the time I reach normal retirement age, I hope to have completed all this. There should be a rental income to me of £25,000.

Cash flow forecasts for the years 1987/88 and 1988/89 are enclosed (Illustrations 11 and 12).

For the year 1987/8, which has already started and for which some of the figures in the cash flow forecasts are 'actual', it will be seen that, apart from the capital expenditure, there is likely to be a cash surplus of £3,000. In the following year, when the benefits of the projected extension come through, the cash surplus increases to £15,000.

I do not need to draw any money for myself out of the enterprise during this two-year period as, for the time being, I have other income resources.

Wagbatch Marina

Cash Flow Forecast 1988–1989

	Oct	Nov	Dec	Jan	Feb	March	April	May	June	July	August	Sept	Total
Moorings (No)	4	35	4	2	0	0	2	37	5	1	0	0	90
Mooring rents		460	4025	460	230	0	0	230	4255	575	115	0	10350
Licences	100	100	0	0	100	130	130	130	130	130	130	100	1180
Sales-gas	102	189	197	213	184	225	210	190	90	20	20	100	1740
Sales-shop	0	0	0	0	0	0	250	700	750	1250	1750	700	5400
Total revenue	202	749	4222	673	514	355	590	1250	5225	1975	2015	900	18670
Licences	95	95	95			95	124	124	124	124	124	124	1124
Purchases	0	0	0			0	450	544	750	1125	919	263	4051
Purchases-gas	85	161	167	181	156	191	179	162	77	17	17	85	1478
Rent BWB			1125			1125			1125			1125	4500
Rates	50	50	50	50			52	52	52	52	52	52	512
Insurance	125												125
Repairs							150	150	150				450
Professional fees						690							690
Interest			82			31			78			514	705
Capital payments									1150	6900	6900	6900	21850
VAT payable	26			673			0			426			1125
Total payments	381	306	1519	904	156	2132	955	1032	3506	8644	8012	9063	36610
Balance	−179	443	2703	−231	358	−1777	−365	218	1719	−6669	−5997	−8163	−17940
Opening bank	−3215	−3394	−2951	−248	−479	−121	−1898	−2263	−2045	−326	−6995	−12992	−12992
Closing bank	−3394	−2951	−248	−479	−121	−1898	−2263	−2045	−326	−6995	−12992	−21155	−21155

Illustration 11

Wagbatch Marina

Cash Flow Forecast 1989–1990

	Oct	Nov	Dec	Jan	Feb	March	April	May	June	July	August	Sept	Total
Moorings (No)	20	53	15	7	0	0	20	53	15	7	0	0	190
Mooring rents		2300	6095	1725	805	0	0	2300	6095	1725	805	0	21850
Licences	200	200	0	0	190	250	250	250	260	250	240	190	2280
Sales-gas	200	300	350	375	350	425	425	350	175	50	20	100	3120
Sales-shop	0	0	0	0	0	0	350	900	900	1500	2500	1000	7150
Total revenue	400	2800	6445	2100	1345	675	1025	3800	7430	3525	3565	1290	34400
Licences	95	190	190	0	0	181	238	238	238	247	238	228	2083
Purchases	0	0	0	0	0	0	600	675	900	1500	1313	375	5363
Purchases-gas	85	255	298	319	298	361	361	298	149	43	17	85	2569
Rent BWB			1125			1125			1125			1125	4500
Rates	52	52	52	52			55	55	55	55	55	55	538
Insurance	250												250
Repairs							250	250	250				750
Professional fees						690							690
Interest			616			460			500			235	1811
Capital payments	1150												1150
VAT payable	−2792			1087			276			1143			−286
Total payments	−1160	497	2281	1458	298	2817	1780	1516	3217	2988	1623	2103	19418
Revenue balance	1560	2303	4164	642	1047	−2142	−755	2284	4213	537	1942	−813	14982
Opening bank	−21155	−19595	−17292	−13128	−12486	−11439	−13581	−14336	−12052	−7839	−7302	−5360	
Closing bank	−19595	−17292	−13128	−12486	−11439	−13581	−14336	−12052	−7839	−7302	−5360	−6173	

Illustration 12

Example 9

Note. The following example is not intended as a description of a possible technical proposition but to show how such a proposition might be planned and presented.

Bradfield Tectonics Ltd

The above company is seeking further capital of £100,000 to increase production of its seismic detection apparatus.

History

Bradfield Tectonics Ltd was formed in 1985 with a capital of 1,000 shares of £1 each; 900 of these shares are held by the managing director, K J Allen, BA (Cantab), PhD (London), and the other 100 by Professor Boothaway of the Department of Geophysics at Bradfield University.

The company's object was to develop an improved seismic detector, as specified by Professor Boothaway. His work on the local geological phenomenon known as the Duffton fault, and later on the far more active Santa Isabel fault in Mexico, is well known. His research in this field persuaded him of the need for a more sensitive seismic detector, encompassing, if possible, some directional capability.

The problem was referred to Dr Allen, at that time Reader in Scientific Instrumentation at Calderwood University. Dr Allen produced a solution to the problem, and in 1985 the company was formed to develop the project and produce the instrument concerned.

Research and development in the first year was funded in part by a loan of £10,000 from Dr Allen (convertible at any time into ordinary shares in the company at par value), in part by a government research grant, and in part by Bradfield University in return for an option to subscribe for 20 per cent of the company's ordinary shares at any time before 31 December 1992, at par or net asset value per share, whichever is the greater.

The accounts for the two years ended 30 September 1987 are enclosed as Appendix A.

There was no production in the first year, which showed a loss of £9,237. In the second year six instruments were completed and sold (all for export) at an ex-works price of £32,000 each. This produced a tiny net profit for the year of £789. The staff then consisted of Dr Allen himself, an electronics production engineer and two workmen, one skilled, one semi-skilled. The company concentrated on assembly and quality assurance, relying on sub-contractors for parts and sub-assemblies.

Enclosed is an account by Professor Boothaway of the geophysical principles and technicalities involved (Appendix B).

The market

On 1 October 1987 the company had an order book for 10 instruments, together with virtually certain orders for a further 12. Steps had already been taken to increase production capacity, both in consultation with the company's suppliers and its own training programme. At that very time the market situation was transformed because of a paper read by Professor Wu of the Wei University, China, at the International Seismological Conference held in Djakarta in September 1987. The subject of Professor Wu's paper was 'Predictive Uses of Small Earth Movements', which demonstrated how the profile of small earth movements could be used to predict earthquakes of Richter Scale 5 or more, provided the data were sufficiently accurate as to scale and location. The instrument Bradfield Tectonics is producing is the only one capable of this accuracy at present on the market.

Visits undertaken by both Dr Young and Professor Boothaway to the authorities in Japan and California have produced letters of intent for the purchase of 80 instruments.

The directors are satisfied that a wide and expanding demand for the product exists in all areas of the world where earthquakes can be expected.

The directors
Kenneth Jackson Allen, managing director, aged 37.

Dr Allen obtained first class honours in Physics at Cambridge in 1971. He obtained a PhD for research at the Imperial College of Science in 1973. From 1973 to 1983 he was with Faraday Electric plc, eventually becoming marketing controller for the Instruments Division. In 1983 he was offered the post of Reader in Scientific Instrumentation at Calderwood. He resigned his Readership in 1985 to set up Bradfield Techtonics.

Anthony Kevin Spooner, BSc (London), aged 31.

Anthony Spooner obtained a degree in Physics. He is also a member of the Institute of Electrical Engineers. A former junior colleague of Dr Allen at Faraday Electric plc, Anthony was offered, in 1979, a position with Supersonic Instruments Inc, becoming production manager at that company's plant in Columbus, Ohio in 1985. Improving conditions and tax levels in the UK and the challenge of the new product have lured him back to England. He will take up the position of production director when his contract with Supersonic ends in two months' time.

The company's accountants are Smith, Brodsky and Toole, 6 Lomas Street, Bradfield.

The company's solicitors are Fifield and Partners, Sepulchre Chambers, Bradfield.

The product
Appendix C contains a full description of the product and its technological specifications.

Essentially it consists of three highly sensitive earth tremor detectors to be located approximately 500 metres apart and connected by cable. Of the three stations, one, the master station, is equipped with sufficient microchip software to correlate the data from all the detectors and to locate, by triangulation, the epicentre of the disturbance.

Short-term policy
So far production has been carried on in a small workshop under the Sheltered Workshop Scheme operated by Bradfield City Council. Already the accommodation has proved to be utterly inadequate. The company has arranged to buy the lease on a factory on the Enterprise Estate, Witherspool, which should prove large enough to meet requirements for some time to come.

The recruitment and training of staff will be of vital importance. The production engineer employed at present is young and his experience is limited, but he is keen and capable, and the company proposes to send him on a course and promote him to assembly shop manager. Four more production workers will be needed, and these will be trained by the company, a training grant having been negotiated with the county council.

The next problem will be the recruitment of service engineers. The company offers its customers a maintenance contract. Maintenance is bound to be expensive because of the travelling involved, and so a substantial margin is being built into the company's costings to cover after-sales service and contingencies. The sums are credited to a 'Maintenance and Service Reserve', and this will be debited with any service charges or fault claims exceeding the fees charged for maintenance. To date, what little maintenance has been required has been carried out by Dr Allen himself and combined with sales visits to potential clients. However, for the future two service engineers willing to travel wherever needed are being recruited and trained.

A chartered or certified accountant to take charge of the financial side is also being recruited.

A micro computer is being acquired on which to keep the accounts. It will also carry a database of all customers and potential customers, as well as records of units sold, together with all the information concerning the performance of each instrument.

Long-term strategy

At present the company is very much a one-product organisation. The sudden opening up of the market means that in the short term the policy must be to exploit this opportunity to its full extent. The company's production plans and marketing drive have had to be brought forward; hence the present demand for capital.

Techtonics Ltd enjoy a special relationship with the Bradfield University Department of Geophysics, and in the longer term the company's aim is to become research-based. Its expertise will be in instrumentation, and its budgeting for the future envisages applying 10 per cent, at least, of gross turnover to Research and Development.

Financial considerations

Dr Allen and Professor Boothaway together will subscribe for a further 29,000 ordinary shares, pro rata to their existing holdings.

Anthony Spooner has agreed to invest £25,000 in the company for a 25 per cent shareholding, ie 10,000 shares, at a price of £2.50 each.

Accordingly, the share capital will be:

		£
Dr Allen	27,000 shares	27,000
Professor Boothaway	3,000 shares	3,000
A Spooner	10,000 shares	10,000
Share Premium Account		15,000
Shareholders' Funds		£55,000

The company is seeking to raise a further £100,000 in long-term finance, either by a loan, convertible loan stock, or by means of a mixed issue of loan and equity.

The additional funds will be used as follows:

	£
Premium on lease	20,000
Machinery and test equipment	50,000
Office equipment and computer	15,000
Motor cars	20,000
Working capital	49,000
	£154,000

Dr Allen and A Spooner will receive a salary of £25,000 a year each, plus bonuses on profits and share options as set out in the draft service agreements (Appendix D).

Profit and loss, cash flow, and balance sheet forecasts are enclosed (Appendix E).

Chapter 7
The Market

That the size and availability of the market is of major importance to the budding entrepreneur was emphasised in Chapter 1.

However good your product or service and however well managed your business, you will never achieve success unless:

1. You have a market of adequate size
2. You have identified your customers
3. You know what they really want
4. You know how to reach them.

The marketing history of one Bruce Entwistle can be used to illustrate the above points.

Bruce had invented a simple little kitchen gadget. Having made a prototype, he carried out some basic market research as to its acceptability to the end-user. What he did was to ask as many housewives as he could contact whether they would be prepared to buy one and how much they would pay. Having satisfied himself that the product would sell, he considered the next step.

The housewives of Great Britain obviously could not be his direct customers. He could not make a living by going from door to door with his inexpensive little gadget. The costs of tooling up for production meant that he would have to sell the gadget in tens of thousands to make a profit.

Now, selling large quantities of any line costs a lot of money, however it is done. Bruce was going to be hard pushed to cover the tooling-up costs for production, so he had to reject ideas such as employing a team of door-to-door salesmen or starting a mail order campaign. He had to reject, too, the idea of selling through individual retail shops. The shopkeepers could not be his direct customers either, as it would be far too expensive to set up the necessary organisation and employ sales representatives.

Eventually he decided to approach the buyers of one or two chain stores. They were interested. They told him what modifications they wanted made to his design and what terms of sale and delivery they required. He negotiated sufficient orders to set up his business and go into production.

Bruce Entwistle had fulfilled the criteria set out above:

1. He had satisfied himself that there was an adequate market among the housewives of the UK
2. He had identified his customers as the buyers of kitchen items for the big retailing multiples
3. He had made his product and terms acceptable to those customers
4. He had found a path of distribution to his end-users.

Let us consider how the people in our examples tackled the market:

The situation of Alexander Battersby (*Example 1*) was relatively simple. He knew there was a market in Ourtown for joinery. His uncle George had been earning a living as a joiner for many years, and Alexander was taking over his business. Alexander knew there was competition but trusted in his skill to meet it. One can criticise him on two counts: first, because he did not make himself aware of his customers' feelings (see Chapter 10), and, second, because his efforts to sell his services were not sufficiently positive, relying too much on word of mouth and a rather vague advertising policy.

Rosemary and Muriel (*Example 2*) had done their homework on the market before they made their decision to start. They selected the sort of customers they thought would buy their product and went out and met some of them. They not only confirmed that the market was there, but actually got some firm orders. One would not expect marketing to be their major problem.

Nicola Grant (*Example 3*) had her market defined for her. It consisted of the customers coming into Mr and Mrs Smith's grocery shop. Her problem resolved itself into deciding whether this market, or even a practicable extension of it, would be large enough to pay her overheads and yield a sufficient profit. Nicola decided it would not.

If Nicola had been intending to open a new shop rather than to buy an existing one, she would have had to involve herself in much more elaborate procedures, ie finding out how many shops were selling her type of goods in the area, how many possible customers passed the door of the premises she had in mind, etc.

Robert Herrick and Deidre Williams (*Example 4*), buying Lamplights Electrical Store, were acquiring a ready made market; but, at the same time, they were going to invest a lot of money in expanding one aspect of the existing business. Robert was already in the trade and knew the local scene well, but he still went to the trouble of visiting 30 out of 49 of his potential customers. He was able to make an estimate of the total trade available to him. His contacts convinced him that he would be able to obtain a sufficient proportion of that trade.

Rita Fairhurst (*Example 7*) was in a very similar position. She, too, had been engaged in the local trade in her product and was aware of the potential. She also undertook a canvass of her possible customers. She made a good assessment of the total market immediately available to her. However, she was not able, as was the electrical goods firm, to obtain such good assurances of future business. The follow-up in Chapter 10 shows that her estimates of the market were too optimistic, and she had to struggle in consequence.

The market research of the inventor, Marcus Garside (*Example 5*), was necessarily more perfunctory. He knew there was a need for an improved seat-belt reel, but he had to take a chance that there would be a market for his particular product when he had designed it and that there would be a customer for his patent.

The makers of the left-handed snooker cues (*Example 6*) carried out a more elaborate market research programme than any other described in this book. James Turbotte did his desk research on the number of left-handed persons. He then set in train a formal quantitative market canvass to find the number of potential users of left-handed cues. Finally, he researched his method of distribution and decided to use Galligaskin and Breeks.

Examples 8 and 9, the expanding businesses, have half their problem solved in that, since they have been successful so far, one can assume that the market is adequate. However, the reader of a business plan must be convinced that the available market is large enough to sustain the expanded business and that it is not moving either to saturation or towards a new fashion.

J S Brook (*Example 8*) has two supports for his belief in the

Wagbatch Marina. He knows that in the previous year the demand was greater than the supply because he had to turn away potential customers, and he knows that the number of boats needing berths is going up at present by 5 per cent each year. (According to the best estimates available, the limit of canal capacity will not be reached until the year 1995.)

As far as marketing is concerned, Bradfield Tectonics Ltd (*Example 9*) is in a very special position. The need for expansion and finance has arisen from a sudden increase in demand for the product. The company will still have need of an active marketing policy, but a shortage of sales is not likely to be the chief problem in the foreseeable future.

All the people in our examples, except possibly Marcus, the inventor, had to be sure that there was a market. They knew that unless they had enough customers there would be no profit for them. They did not proceed on pure hope or a simple faith in the value of their product or service; nor did they place much reliance on the encouragement of their friends. The examples show the means they employed to find out, as best they could, whether an adequate market did, or did not, exist.

Chapter 8
Planning the Borrowing

Many firms go under through bad planning of their finances. It would be tragic if, with all your management skill, and with a large market for a fine product or service, you were to fail at the last because of money problems.

There are businesses that have come into being and have flourished without any money being raised except the proprietors' own. Sturdily independent, even in the raising of finance, the owners have sacrificed rapid growth for the security which owing nothing to anyone brings.

But this chapter will assume that either you cannot 'go it alone' as regards the money, or that you believe your opportunity should be exploited more rapidly than self-financing could possibly achieve. So you have decided to take the risk of borrowing.

Now you must decide what is the most efficient way of borrowing and how much you can risk. Again, your best guide when making your decision is the cash flow forecast you are preparing as an essential part of your business plan.

Take the simplest of our examples first. Alexander Battersby (*Example 1*) needs money to get started, but his cash flow forecast shows him that he will not need it for long, and he intends always to be in the black at the bank thereafter, barring accidents. His customers pay him in cash, so once he has paid off his starting loan, that should be that. Alexander needs only a simple overdraft facility. To take out a term loan would be inappropriate, as Alexander would go on paying interest on the balance even when his current account was in the black – which would be nice for the bank, but not so good for Battersby & Co.

Rita Fairhurst's situation (*Example 7*) is quite different. When Alexander did a job, he got paid for it right away. He even managed to buy half his materials on credit, so the more jobs he got, the faster the money rolled into his bank account. Not so for Rita. For every contract she undertook, she had to pay out wages to her workers for days, or even weeks, before she could send out an invoice; and even then there was a delay before she was paid. The money she needs to lay out on producing the goods before getting paid is termed 'working capital'.

As Rita builds up her business, her need for working capital increases. Some of it will come from the profits that the contracts earn, but not until such profits have covered the overheads and the cash which Rita has to draw to live on. So Rita has to borrow over a longer period, and she has to be sure that the money is available as required. She does not want to have to make repeated calls on the bank manager. She will try, therefore, to negotiate a term loan, with as long a 'holiday' as possible before any repayment of principal need be made.

In *Example 2*, Rosemary and Muriel were in an intermediate position. They give the same period of credit to their customers that they obtain from their major suppliers. The only delay in their cash flow will fall between receipt of the invoices for metal and casting and the date on which they can invoice their statues outwards. Their profit margin is good, so sales generate working capital. On the other hand, their overheads are quite heavy, and they are spending money on publicity and on designing and making new moulds.

Rosemary and Muriel's policy must be, therefore, to fight for more production, so that they can sell more statues. Their borrowing reflects this, in that they took out a term loan with a nine-month moratorium on repayment of principal. This allows them the necessary time before profits exceed overheads and new design costs etc.

They also arranged for an overdraft facility to cover any delays in achieving a really positive cash flow. As events showed, this was wise. The Stanislavski delays threw a strain on their cash position, but their solution of the production problem has put them back into credit.

In *Example 3*, Nicola's business planning persuaded her to give up the idea of buying the Smiths' food shop. But let us consider the buyer of a truly profitable retail shop obtained at an economic price.

The essential basis of good retailing is that you buy from your suppliers on credit and sell to your customers for cash (or for cash through a banker's credit card system). Thus your cash flow is likely to be strongly positive, and the more you trade the faster the bank balance builds up – *so long as you control your buying.*

There are two siren voices in a retailer's ear, one saying, 'If you buy in larger quantities you will get a bigger discount', and the other, 'If you extend your range you will reap more sales'. Both assertions are true as far as they go, but both are fraught with danger.

Acting on the first puts in jeopardy the retailer's advantage of buying on credit and selling for cash. Indeed, if you buy for more than two months' sales, the cash flow becomes negative because you have had money 'out' to suppliers for longer than you have had it 'in' from customers.

Acting on the second and increasing your range will not be truly profitable unless the increase in sales is at least proportionate to the increase in the cost of your stock. The ideal policy, as adopted by Marks and Spencer, is to aim for rapid turnover of a limited range of goods.

If you keep your buying under proper control, a retail shop should need no increase in working capital once you have started trading. You ought not to find it difficult to pay for an increase in stock out of increasing profits. Indeed, in you first months your cash flow should be distinctly positive, as you are selling for cash while your first payments for new goods will not be made until the second month. Allow for this in deciding how much you want to borrow on term loan and how much on overdraft.

Because the capital involved in buying a shop – stock, fixtures and goodwill – is usually high in relation to the profits to be earned, you will try to negotiate terms to repay the loan over several years; but since your ongoing working requirements should be nil, you ought to be able to start repaying almost at once.

If, in addition to buying the business, you are buying the property and can raise the money to do so, my advice is to look upon the two purchases as separate propositions. The one is a venture in retail trade, the other a speculation in shop property. One could prove worthwhile and the other not, depending on circumstance. A separate financing of the property on a long-term basis should be your aim.

When it comes to the Wagbatch Marina (*Example 8*), the means employed to raise the finance for its extension are even simpler and more straightforward.

John Brook has borrowed money to build up an income-generating asset. As long as he can let his berths, the money will roll in, steadily increasing the cash flow. He will arrange a term loan, to be paid off in instalments, these to begin as soon as the berths are ready for letting.

In the five examples discussed so far in this chapter, the financing problems were fairly cut and dried. The obvious resource was some form of bank loan which could be covered by collateral.* What remained to be discussed, though important, was simply the willingness of the bank to lend, the form of the loan and the rate of repayment.

If your fund-raising problem is similar to one of those discussed above, then go to several banks to get the best terms offered. Two rules apply:

1. Take along a copy of your cash flow forecast when you go to negotiate repayment terms.
2. Take care not to agree to earlier repayments than you will be able to make without difficulty.

Incidentally, if you are thinking of taking out a mortgage on your house to raise finance, it is worth considering an approach to your building society. It may be able to give you a better deal than the bank is prepared to offer.

The projects introduced as *Examples 4, 6* and *9* are larger and the financing more complex. None of the companies could offer sufficient collateral to cover the amount of money needed, even if it were appropriate to obtain the entire sum as a loan from the bank.

Anyone making such a loan to one of these companies would be running a risk, as the company might very well fail. Companies do fail, all too frequently. The lenders of unsecured money have to cover their losses on the failures out of the profits they make on the winners. This pushes the interest rate on a straight, unsecured loan up to the 30 per cent mark for all but the most thoroughly researched and copper-bottomed propositions. No responsible bank or similar institution would want to lend to Ourtown Turbotte or Bradfield Tectonics at 30 per cent. The interest rate itself would cripple almost any business. In fact, many businesses

* When you borrow money, you are under a personal obligation to pay it back. The bank will require a guarantee, however, beyond your personal word. This could take the form of a second mortgage on your house, the assignment of an insurance policy, or a signed undertaking by a property-owner prepared to repay the loan should you be unable to do so.

are pushed into liquidation by the horrific cash flow burdens placed on them by high rates of interest and harsh loan repayment terms.

The government, aware of the problem, has instituted the Loan Guarantee Scheme (LGS). Under this, the government itself acts as guarantor to the bank for 70 per cent of the money the bank lends, and the loan can be made without requiring personal security. There are two snags. First, because there is no security, the rate of interest is higher (at present 3 per cent above normal bank lending rate) and, second, since the bank is still lending 30 per cent of the loan without security it scrutinises LGS propositions much more closely than it does requests for ordinary secured loans.

Your best course, if you want to avoid these high interest rates, is to find a source of 'equity' capital.

What does the term 'equity' mean? Originally, of course, it referred to even-handed dealing. Next it was used by lawyers to mean a system of justice which supplemented the rules of the Common Law of the old traditional courts. By derivation it has come to mean, in financial contexts, actual ownership of part of a company, as distinct from merely lending money to it. An ordinary shareholder actually owns part of the company. If 10,000 shares in a company are issued and you own 100 of these, you own 1 per cent of the company. Ordinary shares are, therefore, 'equity' shares.

In general, all ordinary shares are of equal value and have equal rights; but it is legally possible to have ordinary shares which have lesser rights, say as regards voting, as long as they are issued on that understanding. However, both the Stock Exchange and some government departments dislike such distinctions and discrimination.

There are some shares which have a mixed or disguised nature. The wit of financial man has invented all sorts of 'mixed' investment, either to meet special needs or to help with tax problems. Preference shares are really loan stock pretending to be shares. They come in several flavours. There are 'participating' preference shares, which are a kind of half-breed. They have a fixed interest element, like as loan, plus a little share in the profits, like ordinary shares. They are said to have some 'equity element'. Some preference shares or loan stock are given the title 'convertible'. This usually means that they can, according to the rules laid down at their birth, undergo a sex-change, as it were, and become equity in the form of ordinary shares. These non-standard shares are tricky and are best avoided by most small companies. If your company wants to consider issuing such shares, it is essential that you seek expert advice.

But issuing ordinary shares to sell part of the equity is common enough, though there are people who object strongly to 'selling part of my company'. Some even see it as 'giving it away'. If this attitude is based on an overwhelming desire for independence at all costs, that is a personal view and no one can quarrel with it. But if it is grounded in a determination to make as much money as possible and keep the lot, that is greedy – and foolish as well. There is a good deal to be said for selling equity – provided you can get satisfactory terms.

The person, company or bank lending you money is entitled to interest and the return of the money in the proper time. This is true – come profit, come loss, come positive cash flow, come negative cash flow. Inconvenient or even ruinous to you though it may be, the lender must get his money. Not so your equity shareholder. He is with you through thick and thin, in good times or in bad. He can only get his money when you do, and in proportion to his shareholding. A good equity shareholder is an excellent source of finance. Treat him well. Psychologically he is taking a greater risk than you are. You are in control of the joint enterprise. Remember how much more jittery you are in the passenger seat of a car than when you are doing the driving. So don't begrudge him his share of the profits.

But where are these providers of equity capital to be found?

Most prudent people are very chary of buying minority shareholdings. They know only too well that whoever owns 50.1 per cent of a company's shares, effectively controls it as far as day-to-day running is concerned; and anyone holding more than 75 per cent can even alter the company's rule-book, the Articles of Association.

When you are looking for people to invest in your business, only family friends and existing business associates who trust you are likely to put their money your way. Unless, that is, you go to a first-class commercial lawyer who can devise a scheme for giving your minority shareholders protection.

'But where,' you may ask, 'are these venture capital companies we hear so much about?'

Venture capital companies do exist, and some of them deserve the name. Whole books have been written about venture capital, and it is not possible in one chapter of a book on business plans to do more than offer one or two general comments.

Such companies can be divided up, variously, as follows:

1. Those that will invest in new start-ups
2. Those that will not
3. Those that will help, indeed insist on helping, in management
4. Those that have a 'hands-off' approach
5. Those that genuinely offer 'risk' money
6. Those that are purely money-lenders.

What virtually all of them have in common, however, is an inability to help the business which needs anything less than £70,000.

There are two very good reasons for this: The first is the cost of investigating your proposition. The venture capital company does not know you from Adam. It is unlikely to know much, of itself, about the sort of business you are proposing. All it knows is that you have written a good business plan. So now experts have to be paid to check out your proposal. Their investigation may cost as much as £5,000. On an investment of £100,000 over five years, that £5,000 represents only 1 per cent per annum. But on a loan of merely £20,000, it comes to 5 per cent per annum. There is a further point to be taken into consideration, ie that these costs are incurred even if the venture capital company should decide against advancing the money. The successful loans have to cover such costs too. It is easy to see why these companies are not willing to lend sums of less than £70,000.

The second reason is that a small start-up company is deemed unlikely to have sufficient all-round management skills. The only venture capital company likely to be interested is one which has a definite 'hands-on' approach and will expect to have a say in the management. This is not necessarily a bad deal for a new company, but the costs are too great to make an investment of less than £70,000 by the venture capital company worthwhile.

It is apparent that a big funding gap exists below the investment level of £70,000 and above the level at which it is possible to obtain secured bank loans on reasonable repayment terms. This gap is an acknowledged one, not least by some government agencies, and discussions are underway with the aim of finding solutions to the problem. Some local initiatives are in operation, as, for instance, the St Helens Trust. Your local enterprise agency will be able to tell you whether an organisation of this kind is to be found in your area.

Such equity funding as is available often comes with offers of, or insistence upon, management support in one field or another. This is not to be spurned or despised. Few companies have no weaknesses in their management portfolio of skills, and if such an offer is made, it should be given serious consideration. It is not recommended that you be indiscriminate in accepting such offers of assistance. Some are far from disinterested and, at best, agreeing to take on a partner is like accepting a marriage proposal: you have to be sure that you will get on, not only when it is warm and the moon is shining over a calm tropical sea, but on a cold, wet Monday morning in Witherspool, when the bills are coming in through the letter-box.

Let us consider how our three remaining companies (*Examples 4, 6* and *9*) tackled the problem of raising finance.

The directors of Ourtown Electrical Supplies Ltd came up with an ingenious ploy. Making use of the government's Business Expansion Scheme (BES), they approached potential customers and invited them to invest in their enterprise. Under the terms of this scheme, the well-to-do and fairly well-to-do can invest in a small company and have the amount of their investment deducted from their gross income for tax assessment. It appeals, naturally, to the higher tax-rated. They have to keep this money in for five years, and there are other conditions and restrictions.

If you want to consider raising money under the BES, you must consult an accountant experienced in this field. Certainly, it is an excellent way of financing a business. It is cheap compared with venture capital investment and has no cash flow disadvantage until the five years are up. It is not easy, however, to find BES investors for a small firm, especially in a start-up situation. In the case of Ourtown Electrical Supplies Ltd, the investors knew the extent of the market and, indeed, were themselves a substantial part of it. Their belief in the company's success had a self-fulfilling element. Good luck to them!

Turbotte Manufacturing Ltd (*Example 6*) took the Guaranteed Loan Scheme line and obtained the money needed. The loan was a little more expensive than they would have liked, and it must be repaid in due course.

If the company's long-term plans work out, in a few years Turbotte will be coming back for a second tier of finance, probably from 3is (Investors in Industry, as it was), a venture capital fund or a merchant bank.

The Bradfield Tectonics Company is large enough to be able

to approach a venture capital company or a merchant bank. It will choose carefully whom to approach. Some venture capital firms have special interests, and one with a 'high-tech' bias is more likely to be willing to invest. There are others which are really only interested in quick capital gains. They can bring pressure on a successful company to be taken over or to go on to the Unlisted Securities Market (USM). Dr Young and his colleagues may not want this and should avoid such firms.

This chapter is not intended to be a comprehensive account of the ways in which an individual or firm can raise money but an attempt to show how your method of financing your business must be related to its size, its nature and your plans for its future. When you talk to your financial advisers now, I hope it will be with a clearer idea of what you require and how to go about getting it.

Chapter 9
How Not to Write a Business Plan –
or Run a Business

A business plan, to succeed in its aim of raising money, must persuade the reader that four main aspects have been properly covered. It must show:

- that a sufficient market exists
- that the management will be capable and efficient
- that the product or service is good
- that the finance will be adequate to meet requirements and reasonable contingencies.

Your business plan should demonstrate all-round strength and competence. Exhibiting brilliance in one or two aspects is not enough.

The Duke of Wellington, to cite an example from history, has never been rated a 'brilliant' general. He was, however, extremely successful, never lost a battle and lived to an honoured old age. When asked for the secret of his success, he said he never neglected any detail, however small, that might contribute to victory.

The Iron Duke's principle can be applied equally well to running a business. The Duke knew that training, feeding and supplying his troops and paying due attention to the other aspects of running an army were at least as important as the tactics employed in battle. He could perhaps be better described as a successful managing director of his army than as a military genius.

Following the Duke's maxim, your business plan should cover not only the exciting aspects of the business, but the humdrum and tedious ones as well. It is not necessary to set out in detail who will send out statements or make the tea or make sure that the corridors are clean; but the reader of the business plan must be made to feel that somebody will be responsible for dealing efficiently with these matters.

Two business plans I read recently illustrate how one can get carried away and allow one aspect to dominate one's thinking to the exclusion of almost everything else. Both these plans had been written by persons of superior education but neither would have persuaded any worldly-wise financier to invest his money. While both men were full of fire and enthusiasm for their separate projects, neither gave space to the more mundane problems of management and administration, so that the resulting plans were hopelessly unbalanced.

Below are described in some detail the weaknesses of both these plans, but in such a way, of course, that neither can be identified.

The first example came straight out of one of our major universities. The author was clearly fascinated by the technological breakthrough that he believed his colleagues had made. He wrote pages about the advances in solid state physics that had made the project feasible. He very carefully referenced his claims from the scientific point of view, but it was not until he came to page 4 that mention was made of ways in which this technical or scientific breakthrough might be applied in any commercial sense. And even then, commercial application seemed to slip in as a side issue, and this despite the fact that the author was hoping to receive considerable sums of money for development and research.

The next few pages were devoted to describing some interesting ideas the technologists had in mind, but there was no indication as to how the research and development, when completed, could be turned into a profit-making enterprise.

A formal cash flow was given at the end of the document, but this seemed little more than a ritual exercise. The figures used had no apparent derivation from anything in the rest of the 'plan'.

One of the large markets to be targeted was a nationalised industry, but no consideration seemed to have been given to the problems of penetrating the purchasing hide of such an organisation. Some very interesting and credible figures were given for the saving that would accrue to the nationalised industry by the introduction of the new technology, but no thought was given to overcoming the tremendous resistance there would be to the far-reaching changes that its adoption would certainly bring about. In fact, no serious consideration had been given to the marketing of the product and only the vaguest thoughts to its manufacture.

This might almost be given as a classic case of enthusiasm for a technological advance running far, far ahead of the commercial considerations involved. To summarise the mistakes made in this business plan:

1. Far too much technical information was given, little of which would be comprehensible to the reader.
2. No clear line of development was given, nor was a profit forecast. The days have long gone since boards of directors and others were prepared to shell out large sums of money on the say-so of technologists who were 'baffling them with science'.
3. The applicants did not start by describing the market for their product, so there was nothing to excite the interest of the money-men unless and until they first waded through pages of physics.
4. The names of the distinguished scientists who had done the research were mentioned, but there was no indication as to who would be running the enterprise, nor any hint that a management structure had been thought about.

There was no plan of action at all, save to do some more developmental research. Some technological innovation, doubtless excellent of its kind, an awareness of a large potential market for at least one product, and a plea for more funds do not constitute even the beginning of the sort of business plan likely to attract commercial finance. Perhaps, with a major shift in emphasis from the technology to the potential product itself and its market, and with an improvement in clarity, this document could have been used to sell the idea to an existing firm for, say, a payment in royalties. But as a plan designed to show how a company would operate and make use of the money being sought, it was utterly useless.

The second example of an upmarket, blundering business plan is more commercially sophisticated. However, it does share one grievous fault with the first example. This case involved biological technology in which quite a few people have at least a grounding in the basic science. And yet, while reading the first few paragraphs, you wondered what the author was talking about. It could be gathered there was a market for some kind of product, but so many newly minted terms had been used that it took a real effort to translate the text into comprehensible English.

Excessive use of technical terms or jargon is a disease not only of high science and technology. All professions, sports or trades – be they butcher or baker or candlestick-maker – use or develop words with special meanings. Sometimes these words constitute a useful form of shorthand for a new idea; but too many are mere variants, intended to impress or baffle the outsider. Such technical terms or jargon phrases should not be used in a business plan, at least not without some explanation of their meaning. You are not trying to dumbfound your reader, but to show him your clear grasp of the situation.

Let us return to our second bad example – the biotechnological enterprise. The faults here were not limited to an over-indulgence in jargon when writing the formal plan. They ran deeper. The plan displayed a fundamental imbalance in the way the company and its problems were perceived. Originally formed to supply goods to a market thirsting for the products, the company had been on the verge of foundering due to failures of manufacture, both in quality and quantity. It was rescued through the skill and reorganisation effected by a first-class production engineer from another discipline. Now, or so the writers of the business plan appeared to believe, a further injection of capital was all that was needed to ensure the company's future prosperity. The market was taken for granted. The company could sell all it produced, and it was assumed that this happy state of affairs would continue indefinitely. There was in the plan no indication that the company had a marketing policy or that the writers of the plan foresaw the need for one. Nor was there evidence that they had set up a well thought out management structure or any system of financial controls.

One cannot take for granted such matters as who is going to be responsible for what and how the money will be controlled, let alone that a marketing policy will not be needed in the foreseeable future. No one should ever invest money in any concern until satisfied that these aspects have been given adequate consideration and a proper plan has been made to deal with them.

'But,' you may well ask, 'what lessons are there in these two examples for the very small business?' It is true that in both these cases sums of about £250,000 were sought; but the very same problems face the individual about to start on his own with, at the most, part-time help. Indeed, the problem shown in the first example confronts almost every sole entrepreneur who wants to manufacture and sell a product, whatever it may be.

The people who wrote the first plan were not clear what kind of business they wanted to be in. Are you? Let us say that you have decided there is a future in the handcuff business. Now where is your strength? Are you a designer of handcuffs? Or a skilled craftsman or production engineer? Do you, perhaps, through a working life spent with Interpol, know the world market for handcuffs and who the buyers are? Or are you a good manager, with financial and administrative skills, who has seen an opportunity in the handcuff trade? Unless you have pots of money and an already established market, you cannot afford to buy in the management skills you need to supplement your own – that is, if you want to control the whole process, from design to selling the finished product. So choose your line. Either make handcuffs and let someone else sell them; or sell handcuffs and contract out the manufacture to someone else.

Take for example a small manufacturing concern making a first-class, moderately priced engineering product, well thought of in the trade, and with potential for vastly greater sales. It is a very small business: the owner, with some part-time help, does everything himself. And there is his problem. He designed the product, he makes it himself at the bench, he does the selling and the paperwork and writes up the books. He attends business management courses and seminars. He works very hard, and yet the business grows at a snail's pace. In 15 or 20 years, if his health holds and his product is not superseded, he may achieve a reasonable income and no longer have to work 70 hours a week for 50 weeks of the year. As things are, he just cannot bring himself to let go of any part of the business and thus reduce his workload and the number of problems he has to solve.

It is true that there have been men who won fame by building up big businesses from almost nothing. But such people are becoming increasingly rare as business life grows more complicated. Those who succeed in this way must have flair amounting to genius. This book is not aimed at business geniuses; it is intended for those among us of more modest abilities who hope to make the most of what resources we have.

If you have read the business plans of the snooker cue makers and of the two ladies in the garden statuary business, you will have noticed that in neither case do they intend to run everything, from designing to selling, themselves. The statues are going to be fabricated by someone else, and the snooker cues, for the time being, are going to be sold by another firm. The financiers to whom the plans are presented will see that in both cases energy and resources are going to be concentrated where it matters and that, in consequence, the number of day-to-day problems with which the managers will have to grapple will be much reduced.

It is sometimes said that there are just not enough experienced people with management skills to go round. In the USA, the financial houses judge business plans more by the management ability offered than by any other factor, certainly more than by the excellence of the product itself; and they insist that the management must be 'balanced'.

By balanced, they mean that the various aspects of management should not outweigh one another. A business may sometimes be referred to as 'market-led' or, alternatively, 'design-led'. These are jargon terms for a real, though rather vague, concept. What 'market-led' should not mean, however, is that the sales manager makes all the decisions and grabs every order he can lay his hands on while those in charge of production and finance have to struggle desperately and, too often, hopelessly to catch up.

'Design-led' should not mean that the talented designer or design engineer can insist on all his wonderful ideas being put into production despite the protests of the marketing side or the horror expressed by the finance director. Every side of management, whether represented by a separate person or in the compartments of the mind of a sole proprietor, should be able to admonish with a 'Hey, slow up there,' or encourage with a 'Come on, get moving,' and do so effectively.

This is what balanced management is about. Build this balanced management into your plan, and make it clear to the reader of your plan that the balance is there.

The question of balance in management is crucial. That does not mean simply paying proper attention to the design side, to selling and to production. These are the interesting aspects for which everyone sees the need. But the boring side of business is equally vital to success: sound bookkeeping, good stores control etc – in short, all those jobs you did *not* go into business on your own to do. We all know about firms who go bust despite having a fine product and expert salesmen, but whose office and stores administration can only be described as slovenly. They rarely deliver spares in the time promised, fail to answer queries, delay sending out invoices and – before they have grasped what is happening – suddenly find themselves in the hands of the receiver.

To revert to the Iron Duke's maxim, Napoleonic plans of tremendous breadth and vision are fine, but Wellington's attention to detail won the battle of Waterloo.

Chapter 10
Monitoring Progress

In this chapter it is assumed that you have obtained your money from the bank, have started up and are now well into your stride. Perhaps you are doing better than you expected or perhaps worse. Or do you really know how you are doing? You will know if you have followed the advice in Chapter 2 and used your cash flow forecast as a budgetary control. Do you remember what the suggestion was? You were to fill in the 'actual' columns with the figures you actually achieved, thereby keeping abreast of what was happening. You should also have kept a copy, not only of the formal business plan you sent to the bank, but also of the more detailed plan you drew up initially. Constant re-reading of this document keeps you in touch with your original plan.

One of the dangers for the small business man is preoccupation with the day-to-day problems he faces. The more work on hand, the truer this is. From the one-man service trader, working around the clock on a seasonal flush of jobs, to the owner of a factory, struggling to complete a big order, the story is the same: there is no time to think until the latest crisis has been overcome. The danger is that in solving each problem as it arises or, indeed, in grabbing at an opportunity as it occurs, one can get diverted from one's true path almost without realising it.

If you have a partner or a trusted manager, you should be talking to him regularly about the business. You should review your plan at regular intervals – even if you do it alone. Get out your business plan and your latest updated cash flow forecast, then go over all aspects of the business in the light of the figures, so that what needs changing, what needs slowing down, what needs speeding up, and where to go next can be considered and resolved.

It is very useful to have an interested and friendly outsider present at this meeting. The obvious person would be your accountant. The good, modern accountant is no longer content just to prepare accounts at the year end – or some months after – and agree your tax bill with the Inspector. He is eager to give regular help and advice. If you are lucky enough to have a competent, up-to-date accountant, make use of the services he can offer. His fees per hour may sound very high, but his advice may well prove invaluable.

You may decide to call at your local Enterprise Agency to discuss your plans and your hopes and fears. The counsellors there will be delighted to see you, and the service is free. A regular visit at three-monthly intervals, so that your progress can be monitored, is recommended. If the staff cannot come up with an answer to your every question, at least you will be told where you can go for specialist help. And, in any case, just talking about it can often clarify a problem and bring a solution to mind.

There are two other groups of people who will be interested in your success: your main suppliers and your chief customers, with individuals in both groups who, if they themselves are good at what they do, will be pleased to help you become more efficient and prosperous. Visit them regularly. They will prove to be a major source of information, tips and advice. Try to call on them just before you hold your 'mini' directors' meetings, so that their views can be considered too.

In the following pages you will be able to find out how the various characters, whose business plans were described earlier, progressed and developed their ideas. The interesting ones are those starting up in business for the first time. The others can be assumed to be able to look after themselves.

As might be expected, each of the start-up examples runs into one typical sort of problem or another, and you will see how their difficulties are overcome.

Example 1

Alexander Battersby, the skilled joiner, did keep track of how his business was progressing. His job in doing so was made relatively easy because Doreen Gray was looking after his books. Keeping the books bang up to date is the necessary basis of good management, whether the business is a corner shop or a multinational.

You can see on the bank forecast form on pages 124–5 how it worked out for the first six months. The outgoings have been fairly accurately forecast. The motor expenses are a little higher than expected, but Alexander has not had to use any money for contingencies – yet.

On the other hand, Alexander had noticed pretty early on that he was not getting enough work by word of mouth recommendation. He got the expected work from builders, and the DIY rescue work was, if anything, better than forecast, thanks to his friend at the DIY shop; but the private house work was not up to expectation.

Although it was Alexander's long-term plan to develop the sub-contracting side of his business, he could not help worrying about this shortfall in the work on private homes. He knew the jobs he had done were first-class, and yet the householders did not seem to be recommending him to their friends and neighbours.

After three months in the business, Alexander decided to call at the local Enterprise Agency. The Agency counsellor listened to what he had to say, discussed with him ideas for advertising and publicity and then put a few rather searching questions to Alexander:

1. Were there occasions when he did not turn up at the time agreed?
2. Did he ever fail to let the householder know when he could not keep an appointment?
3. Did he sometimes neglect to tidy up after finishing a job?
4. Had he left doors open when going in and out of the house?
5. Did he smoke without first asking permission?
6. Did he keep his transistor radio going full blast?

Despite feeling somewhat resentful at being asked such questions, Alexander had to admit that he had been guilty on most of these counts. On one occasion he had not finished the morning's job by lunch-time and did not let his next customer know because 'it was a bit awkward to phone'. The lady was furious, as she had taken an afternoon off work to see the job done. There was another time when something similar happened. He denied that he had ever left without sweeping up; he took too much pride in his work to allow that. But he did admit that he was a bad one for leaving doors open – his wife was always complaining – and he was a heavy smoker.

The counsellor emphasised that Alexander was in what is called a service industry, and success would depend not just on doing a fine job technically but on pleasing the customers in every way, even if some of them seemed to him unnecessarily fussy.

When the counsellor had a look at the cash flow forecast, he said

National Westminster Bank PLC **Cash flow Forecast For**

Branch   6 High Street, Ourtown   name of company, firm etc

Enter month	January		February		March	
	Projected	**Actual**	Projected	**Actual**	Projected	**Actual**
Receipts						
Sales – Cash	780	771	850	873	850	781
Sales – Debtors						
Loans						
Other receipts	950	950				
A Total receipts	1730	1721	850	873	850	781
Payments						
Cash purchases	51	83	51	48	51	32
To creditors			51	31	51	43
Wages and salaries (net)						
PAYE/NIC						
Capital items	875	875				
Rent/rates	22	22	22	22	22	22
Services					35	35
Professional fees (D. Gray)			50	50	50	50
Bank/finance charges						
Advertising	100	115				30
Motor expenses	30	32	30	43	130	157
Insurance	300	300				
Sundries (& Licences)	150	150	5	11	5	4
Drawings	420	420	420	420	420	420
Contingencies	12		12		12	
B Total payments	1960	1997	641	625	776	793
Opening bank balance	NIL	NIL	−230	−276	−21	−28
Add to B if overdrawn Subtract from B if credit						
C Total	1960	1997	871	901	797	821
D Closing bank balance (Difference between A&C)	−230	−276	−21	−28	53	−40

For the period

Alexander Battersby   From Jan 1988   To June 1988

| April | | May | | June | | **Total** | |
Projected	**Actual**	Projected	**Actual**	Projected	**Actual**	Projected	**Actual**
900	760	950	893	950	1027	5280	5105
						950	950
900	760	950	893	950	1027	6230	6055
54	41	57	51	57	75	321	330
51	44	54	32	57	31	264	181
						875	875
22	22	22	22	22	22	132	132
	10			35	45	70	90
50	50	50	50	50	50	250	250
35	38					35	38
		50	35			150	180
30	45	30	52	130	152	380	382
						300	300
5	8	5	8	5	3	175	184
420	420	420	420	420	420	2520	2520
12		12		12		72	0
679	678	700	670	788	798	5544	5461
53	−40	274	42	524	265		
626	718	426	628	264	533		
274	42	524	265	686	494		

Illustration 13

that if everything went as planned, Alexander would have tax to pay. Fairly big payments might fall due in 18 months or two years' time, which could come as a very nasty surprise if money was not put by in readiness. He suggested that 20 per cent of the turnover in excess of £650 per month should be put into a building society account. Not only would this enable Alexander to pay the tax when it came due, but the savings would be earning interest in the meantime.

As a result of this interview, Alexander mended his ways and, towards the end of six months, found he was getting a good number of jobs through private recommendations. In fact, as the bank forecast shows, his sales in June were better than expected.

Example 2

During the first six months Rosemary and Muriel found themselves in danger of being blown off course due to the Stanislavski Foundry falling behind with its own capacity expansion programme. Not only was production for months 3, 4 and 5 going to be affected, but the planned production for the whole of the year was put at risk.

Muriel drew up a new cash flow schedule for the year. For the first three months she entered what actually had happened; for the next nine the figures were based on the new production forecasts of the foundry, with savings on advertising costs, as it would be no use advertising goods they would not have on hand to sell. The result, as shown in Illustration 14, was not encouraging.

Action was taken immediately. Rosemary and Muriel went to see the managing director of Stanislavski. The meeting was a little stormy. The MD promised to do what he could, but he talked too much about his own difficulties and the cheap price Rosemary and Muriel were paying.

Rosemary then went to call at another foundry in the Bristol area. Here she was given the red carpet treatment, and a contract was signed for four statues a month, production to begin at once, with a promise of four more per month in six months' time.

The new moulds, including the one for the rampant lion (which was proving especially popular), were sent to Bristol.

As soon as the MD of Stanislavski heard of this, he called on Rosemary. He had good news, he said. He had managed to overcome his difficulties, and by the end of the month after next would be able to increase production to five statues per month. In four months' time the foundry would be able to turn out 10 statues per month, and there would be no increase in price.

As the orders had been rolling in, Rosemary and Muriel knew they could sell all they could produce. Their cash flow forecast had to be brought up to date yet again.

This time they would include further costs for design and moulds, as there was a strong demand for a wider range of models and it was obvious they would need some paid help.

At the end of six months the cash flow forecasts were amended once more, this time to show the actual results for the first half year and the improved prospects for the second half. These new forecasts are shown in Illustration 15.

Now Rosemary and Muriel reviewed their business plan in the light of their latest forecasts and the very healthy demand for their statues. They had their accountant from Belt & Braces in on the discussion. It was decided they should:

1. Carry on with the same marketing and advertising procedures
2. Design a larger range of statues (One hotel firm wrote: 'People don't want to see a Copenhagen Mermaid in every foyer throughout England.')
3. Follow up a marketing idea of Muriel's: to make smaller statues for private houses and gardens
4. Employ a full-time assistant, preferably an art college graduate, to enable them to increase production
5. Seek out yet another foundry, both to keep their two existing suppliers on their toes and to provide for further expansion.

The accountant congratulated them on the progress they had made, saying they would soon have a business of which they could be proud.

Example 3

Nicola's business planning had persuaded her, as you will remember, not to start at all. She was glad of this when, some months later, it became obvious that Mr and Mrs Smith's grocery business was going downhill.

However, the exercise of working out the figures and making up her mind to give up a lovely dream had convinced Nicola that she was not as stupid and feeble as she had been made to feel at times in the past.

Before her marriage Nicola had worked in an office, and she decided to take a course at the local College of Adult Education to learn word processing and how to use fax and other modern equipment.

127

Profit and Loss Account

Rosemary Rambler and Muriel Tonks
First Revised Profit and Loss and Cash Flow Forecast
After three months' trading

Profit and Loss Account	Month 1	Month 2	Month 3	Month 4	Month 5	Month 6	Month 7	Month 8	Month 9	Month 10	Month 11	Month 12	Total
Number of statues sold	1	2	2	3	3	3	3	3	3	4	4	4	35
Value of sales	650	1300	1300	1950	1950	1950	1950	1950	1950	2600	2600	2600	22750
less													
Metal and casting	285	570	570	855	855	855	855	855	855	1140	1140	1140	9975
Moulds and design	20	40	40	60	60	60	60	60	60	80	80	80	700
Overheads	964	964	964	964	964	964	964	964	964	964	964	964	11568
Interest	47	47	47	47	47	47	47	47	47	41	41	41	546
Wages													0
Depreciation	67	67	67	67	67	67	67	67	67	67	67	67	804
Profit	-733	-388	-388	-43	-43	-43	-43	-43	-43	308	308	308	-843

Cash Flow Forecast

	Month 1	Month 2	Month 3	Month 4	Month 5	Month 6	Month 7	Month 8	Month 9	Month 10	Month 11	Month 12	Total
Receipts from sales		748	1495	1495	2243	2243	2243	2243	2243	2243	2990	2990	23176
Loans	4000												4000
Other receipts	4000												4000
Total receipts	8000	748	1495	1495	2243	2243	2243	2243	2243	2243	2990	2990	31176
Payments for:													
Metal and casting	0	656	656	983	983	983	983	983	983	1311	1311	1311	11143
Moulding materials	460	460	57	57	230	230	57	57	230	230	57	57	2182
Moulding wages	60	120				60				60			300
Overheads	2219	816	844	1046	529	644	1796	529	644	1046	489	604	11206
Interest			141			141			141			123	546
Other wages													0
Drawings	500	500	500	500	500	500	500	500	500	500	500	500	6000
Capital payments	3600												3600
VAT				−705			178			194			−333
Loan repayments									500			500	1000
Total payments	6839	2552	2198	1881	2242	2558	3514	2069	2998	3341	2357	3095	35644
Balance	1161	−1804	−703	−386	1	−315	−1271	174	−755	−1098	633	−105	−4468
Bank balance	1161	−643	−1346	−1732	−1731	−2046	−3317	−3143	−3898	−4996	−4363	−4468	

Illustration 14

Rosemary Rambler and Muriel Tonks
Second Revised Profit and Loss and Cash Flow Forecast
After negotiating new production contracts

Profit and Loss Account

	Month 1	Month 2	Month 3	Month 4	Month 5	Month 6	Month 7	Month 8	Month 9	Month 10	Month 11	Month 12	Total
Number of statues sold	1	2	2	3	7	9	9	9	10	12	14	14	92
Value of sales	650	1300	1300	1950	4550	5850	5850	5850	6500	7800	9100	9100	59800
less													
Metal and casting	285	570	570	855	1995	2565	2565	2565	2850	3420	3990	3990	26220
Moulds and design	20	40	40	60	140	180	180	180	200	240	280	280	1840
Overheads	962	962	962	962	962	962	962	962	962	962	962	962	11544
Interest	47	47	47	47	47	47	47	47	47	47	47	47	564
Wages									200	200	200	200	800
Depreciation	67	67	67	67	67	67	67	67	67	67	67	67	804
Profit	−731	−386	−386	−41	1339	2029	2029	2029	2174	2864	3554	3554	18028

Cash Flow Forecast

	Month 1	Month 2	Month 3	Month 4	Month 5	Month 6	Month 7	Month 8	Month 9	Month 10	Month 11	Month 12	Total
Receipts from sales		748	1495	1495	2243	5233	6728	6728	6728	7475	8970	10465	58308
Loans	4000												4000
Other receipts	4000												4000
Total receipts	8000	748	1495	1495	2243	5233	6728	6728	6728	7475	8970	10465	66308
Payments for:													
Metal and casting	0	656	656	983	2294	2950	2950	2950	3278	3933	4589	4589	29828
Moulding materials	453	340	0	230	230	230	230	230	230	230	230	230	2863
Moulding wages	65	65				60	250	250	250	250	250	250	1690
Overheads	2192	788	878	1046	529	644	1796	529	644	1046	489	604	11185
Interest			141			141			141			123	546
Other wages									200	200	200	200	800
Drawings	500	500	500	500	500	500	500	500	500	500	500	500	6000
Capital payments	3600								500				
VAT				−705			68						
Loan repayments										1015		500	1000
Total payments	6810	2349	2175	2054	3553	4525	5794	4459	5743	7174	6258	6996	57890
Balance	1190	−1601	−680	−559	−1310	708	934	2269	985	301	2712	3469	8418
Bank balance	1190	−411	−1091	−1650	−2960	−2252	−1318	951	1936	2237	4949	8418	

Illustration 15

131

Nicola has a part-time job now, working in the offices of a firm in Witherspool, and is feeling much more pleased with herself.

Example 4

A loan was successfully negotiated with the Home Counties Bank under the Loan Guarantee Scheme. Unfortunately, there were unforeseen delays over the lease. Redd, Herring and Co for the company and Manyana, Manyana & Holliday for the lessors were unable to complete the formalities, despite extensive and protracted correspondence, until well into the new year.

This delay produced a series of damaging consequences:

1. The company was two months late in launching its comprehensive service to the electrical trade. This gave the competitors from Bradfield an opportunity to ginger up their own services and forestall Ourtown Electrical Supplies Ltd. One firm went so far as to open a branch in Witherspool.
2. Two of the working electricians, who had planned to put up some of the capital under the BES scheme, got fed up and backed out. To make up the shortfall, Mr Lamplight agreed to a delay in the payment to him of a part, ie £4,000, of the sum he was to receive for his stock.
3. The company found itself landed with a large range of fancy electrical gift items which had been ordered for Christmas. (It had been possible to cancel only one or two orders without penalty.) The cash flow position was so bad by the time the Verges Street premises opened that the business there had to be started with a 'Sale'.
4. The publicised gala opening took place at a dead time of year; Bobby Lovebird was no longer able to attend; and the whole affair fell rather flat.
5. The legal arrangements were much more complicated than had been expected, and the legal costs were almost twice what had been budgeted for. Unfortunately, by the terms of the lease, Ourtown Electrical Supplies Ltd had to bear the whole of these costs.

The long-term effects of the delayed opening – through opportunities given to competitors, disappointment suffered by important customers, etc – are hard to assess; but even in the short term the effect on cash flow could have been disastrous if the company had not budgeted for more in the way of financial resources than a strict analysis of requirements demanded.

As it was, the company survived – just. The local electrical contractors remained loyal, and the company has proved itself able to offer a first-class and economical service. The new showroom is beginning to be visited by the public, and this gives hope for retail trade in the future.

Although six months have not yet gone by since the nearly disastrous start, the books show that sales are not far off the original monthly target and, in fact, are growing at a slightly better rate than forecast. Everyone still has hopes of a bright future for the company, though things may never be quite as good as if the delay had not occurred.

The accountants drew up a new profit forecast and cash flow to the end of the year, including the actual results for the first five months (Illustration 16). They assumed that the company would be back on monthly sales target by the end of the year. But the delay over the lease, which could not have happened at a worse time of year, had a dreadful effect, as you can see, on both profit and bank balance.

The moral is that once you are committed to a plan, any delay in getting properly started can be very expensive. In this case it was a legal delay, but it could have been a building contractor's delay, the failure of a financial sponsor to come up with the money on time, non-delivery of machinery, etc. The author knows of an enterprise in which £250,000 had been invested. Because some computer software had not been fully tested and was not running properly until a fortnight after the business was launched, the whole enterprise collapsed and all participants lost their money.

Do not rely on promises of delivery. Allow for some inevitable delays. But do not tell your contractors you are doing so! Otherwise they will take their period of grace and still be late. Have them on a savage penalty clause for delay – if you can.

Example 5

Marcus was very pleased with the way in which production of his prototypes went forward. What is more, the testing showed that his seat belt design was far superior to anything else in its class on the market.

However, now he began to run into difficulties. He had assumed that once he had developed his design and patented it, he would be able to find an agent or broker to help him sell his rights; but no such person or firm could be discovered. His patent agent said that he could not actually help to sell the patent for reasons of

Ourtown Electrical Supplies Ltd
Financial projections for first year's trading
as amended after six months' trading

Profit and Loss Account

	Month 2	Month 3	Month 4	Month 5	Month 6	Month 7	Month 8	Month 9	Month 10	Month 11	Month 12	Month 1	Total
Sales	11858	16455	19509	21867	25492	28202	28100	29600	22200	34000	37000	37000	311283
less													0
Cost of goods sold	8398	12576	14085	15834	18597	20614	20518	21680	16260	24775	27100	27100	227537
Overheads	6373	6373	6373	6373	6373	6373	6373	6373	6373	6373	6373	6373	76476
Interest on overdraft	0	0	0	100	39	19	13	82	73	71	68	53	518
Interest on loan	333	315	298	280	263	245	228	210	193	175	158	140	2838
Depreciation	313	677	677	677	677	677	677	677	677	677	677	677	7760
Net profit	−3559	−3486	−1924	−1397	−457	274	291	578	−1376	1929	2624	2657	−3846
Balance of loan	28500	27000	25500	24000	22500	21000	19500	18000	16500	15000	13500	12000	

Cash Flow Forecast

	Month 12	Month 1	Month 2	Month 3	Month 4	Month 5	Month 6	Month 7	Month 8	Month 9	Month 10	Month 11
Sales-payments	3409	12912	19008	22586	25782	29470	31936	32764	31654	30199	37927	42033
Loans	30000											
Capital introduced	46000											
Total receipts	79409	12912	19008	22586	25782	29470	31936	32764	31654	30199	37927	42033
Purchases payments	2001	19453	14636	16399	18527	21619	23695	23729	24309	19678	28759	31165
Overheads	11504	9323	6612	5906	4197	4887	5756	6760	4887	5656	6455	4582
Interest			945			946			798			663
Drawings	1500	1500	1500	1500	1500	1500	1500	1500	1500	1500	1500	1500
Loan repayments												
Capital items	17250	0	20125	0	0	0	4000	0	0	0	0	0
Opening stock	13000	0	0	0	0	0	0	0	0	0	0	0
VAT	0	0	0	-6138	0	0	2540	0	0	3142	0	0
Total payments	45255	30276	43818	17667	24224	28952	37491	31989	31494	29976	36714	37910
Cash flow	34154	-17364	-24810	4919	1558	518	-5555	775	160	223	1213	4123
Bank												
Opening balance	0	34154	16790	-8020	-3101	-1543	-1025	-6580	-5805	-5645	-5422	-4209
Closing balance	34154	16790	-8020	-3101	-1543	-1025	-6580	-5805	-5645	-5422	-4209	-86

Illustration 16

135

professional ethics; and neither his accountant nor his solicitor knew of any source of help. Two non-profit making organisations were generous with advice, but for actually doing the job of selling his patent Marcus was on his own. Truly, as stated at the beginning of Chapter 6, the path of an inventor is hard – especially in the UK.

Bewildered, but determined, Marcus set about finding a firm to take on his product. Naturally, he tried the local ones first; then others in the UK. All turned him down, giving one reason or another. A marketing organisation, however, was impressed by the product, and one of its directors suggested a deal: if Marcus formed his own company to manufacture the seat-belt, the marketing people, in return for an option to buy a controlling interest at net asset value in three years' time, would do the selling for him. They would even go so far as to find a finance company to help Marcus set up as a manufacturer. Marcus, being a courteous individual, thanked them and politely declined the offer.

In the meantime, Marcus has received two promising offers, one from an Italian company and one from Taiwan. A firm of commercial solicitors in London is negotiating on his behalf, and he has great hopes of a satisfactory arrangement being made.

Example 6

The Turbotte Manufacturing Company Ltd got off to a good start. The Home Counties Bank agreed to the loan, and the company's organisation and methods were working well. Galligaskin and Breeks were selling plenty of cues, production was going as expected, and staff training was proceeding satisfactorily.

However, after four months James Turbotte set off for the antipodes on a marketing survey tour, and in the course of this he made a bad mistake. Infected by the enthusiasm displayed for his product by an Australian company, he signed a contract for a very large order of cues, the production of which his firm would find impossible to finance. His calculations (on the back of an envelope) of the production capacity required, when checked later, were not too far out. By making a big effort and paying considerable overtime, the company could meet the contract without undue disruption of other commitments; but when it came to the required working capital, it was obvious that the money would not be available as needed. James had been careless in agreeing the amount of credit the purchasers would be allowed.

Julian Watchman, the finance director, was furious, and on

James's return to England a very stormy meeting of the directors took place. The company, which had been so successful so far, had reached the limits of its financial resources, and the bank could not, or would not, help. As a last resort, James tried to get the payment terms of the Australian contract revised. The Australians, whom he had found so hospitable, turned out to be tough bargainers, and the extra discount that had to be given almost wiped out the profit on the order.

To tide the company over this bad patch, the directors agreed not to draw their salaries during the crucial months, and the firm has managed to survive. In fact, it now looks forward with renewed confidence to a prosperous future.

Example 7

Rita Fairhurst started out with good orders in hand, so that her first month's sales were satisfactory. But the follow-through orders were disappointing. It was not that her customers were dissatisfied with either the quality of work or the deliveries; the trouble was that Rita did not have time to go out and drum up trade for the months ahead because she was so busy in March and April setting up her workshop and organising her staff. Her competition seized the opportunity and spent time and money in a big effort to obtain orders for the summer months.

By the time Rita realised what was happening, too many orders had been tied up by her rivals, and Rita was unable to maintain the production levels she had hoped for. She called her staff together and explained the position. Most of her workers had long been on friendly terms with Rita and were prepared to stand by her and work short time while she got down to work to canvass for every order she could find.

After six months, the tide began to turn. It was at this time that she brought her cash flow forecast up to date, entering the actual results for the first six months and amending, in the light of experience, the forecast for the second half of the year. (See Illustration 17.)

You will notice the falling turnover during the summer, together with the economy on wages. But you will notice, also, that Rita's sales drive obliged her to spend more on petrol and on printing.

Her campaign produced considerable hope for the future, but Rita was more cautious in estimating both turnover and profit margins than she had been at the start.

Rita Fairhurst

Enter Month		April		May		June		July		August	
Figures rounded to £ 's		Budget	Actual	Budget	Actual	Budget	Actual	Budget	Actual	Budget	Actual
	Receipts										
1	Sales (inc VAT)-Cash			7,245	7,398	7,245	6,721	7,245	5,680	3,622	3,210
2	-Debtors										
3	Other Trading Income										
4	Loans Received	5,000	5,000								
5	Capital Introduced	6,500	6,500								
6	Disposal of Assets										
7	Other Receipts										
A	**Total Receipts**	11,500	11,500	7,245	7,398	7,245	6,721	7,245	5,680	3,622	3,210
	Payments										
8	Cash Purchases										
9	Payments to Creditors										
10	Principals' Remuneration	375	375	375	375	375	375	375	375	375	375
11	Wages/Salaries (net)	3,659	3,710	3,659	3,426	3,659	3,157	2,650	2,132	2,650	1,254
12	PAYE/NI					1,800	1,584				
13	Capital Items	3,450	3,450								
14	Petrol etc	56	76	56	42	56	58	56	96	56	87
15	Rent/Rates	772	772	85	85	85	85	772	772	85	85
16	Services							300	287		
17	Leasing	1,449	1,449			483	483	483	483	483	483
18	Maintenance	174	174	174	174	174	174	174	174	174	174
19	Interest					163	163				
20	Bank/Finance Charges										
21	Professional Fees										
22	Telephone	115	115					126	104		
23	Insurance	250	250								
24	Printing, Sundries	250	285	90	56	90	45	90	106	90	150
25											
26	VAT							1,027	970		
27	Corporation Tax etc										
28	Dividends										
B	**Total Payments**	10,550	10,656	4,439	4158	6,885	6124	6,053	5,499	3,913	2,608
C	**Net Cashflow (A−B)**	950	844	2.806	3,240	360	598	1,192	181	−291	602
29	Opening Bank Balance	0	0	950	844	3,756	4,084	4,116	4,682	5,308	4,863
D	**Closing Bank Balance (C± Line 29)**	950	844	3,761	4,084	4,116	4,682	5,308	4,863	5,017	5,465

138

September		October		November		December		January		February		March		Total	
Budget	Actual	Budget	Actual	Budget	Actual	Budget	Actual	Budget	Actual	Budget	Actual	Budget	Actual	Budget	Actual
3,622	2,840	7,245	6,105	7,245	6,800	7,245	6,800	7,245	6,800	7,245	6,800	7,245	6,800	72,449	65,954
														5,000	5,000
														6,500	6,500
3,622	2,840	7,245	6,105	7,245	6,800	7,245	6,800	7,245	6,800	7,245	6,800	7,245	6,800	83,949	77,454
375	375	375	375	375	375	375	375	375	375	375	375	375	375	4,500	4,500
3,659	3,420	3,659	3,500	3,659	3,500	3,659	3,500	3,659	3,500	3,659	3,500	3,659	3,500	41,890	38,099
1,300	1,153					1,800	1,700					1,800	1,700	6,700	6,137
														3,450	3,450
56	85	56	56	56	56	56	56	56	56	56	56	56	56	672	780
85	85	772	772	85	85	85	85	772	772					3,598	3,598
		300	257					300	300					900	844
483	483	483	483	483	483	483	483	483	483	483	483	483	483	6,279	6,279
174	174	174	174	174	174	174	174	174	174	174	174	174	174	2,088	2,088
162	162					163	163					162	162	650	650
		126	180					126	126					493	525
						325	325							575	575
90	56	90	90	90	90	90	90	90	90	90	90	90	90	1,240	1,238
		1,520	1,146					2,565	2,233					5,112	4,349
6,385	5,994	7,555	7,033	4,922	4,763	7,210	6,951	8,600	8,109	4,837	4,678	6,800	6,541	78,755	73,792
−2,763	−3,154	−310	−928	2,323	2,037	36	−151	−1,355	−1,309	2,408	2,122	446	259		
5,017	5,465	2,254	2,311	1,944	1,383	4,267	3,420	4,303	3,269	2,948	1,960	5,356	4,082		
2,251	2,311	1,944	1,383	4,267	3,420	4,303	3,269	2,948	1,960	5,356	5,265	4,082	5,802	4,341	

(Updated to show actual figures for April to September and revised forecast for remainder of the year)

Illustration 17

139

Chapter 11
Where to Go for Further Advice

Your local Enterprise Agency

This is the natural first port of call for anyone thinking of starting a business.

Enterprise Agencies were founded with the express aim of helping small businessmen, especially those just starting up. They are not government agencies, but have been set up, as a rule, through the joint efforts of local businessmen and local authorities. Usually, the director is someone from a very large company, seconded from the ranks of senior executives. He will be supported by a number of counsellors, probably retired business-men, each with a lifetime's experience to draw on.

The service is free at all levels.

The address of the local Enterprise Agency should be listed in the Yellow Pages or your local directory. If not, try the Citizens Advice Bureau or the Jobcentre.

Your trade association

When you are doing your market research, it is often wise to get in touch with the trade association relevant to your business. It may provide useful statistics and other information and enable you to decide whether there is sufficient potential to give you a chance of success. The local Chamber of Commerce will be able to supply the address.

Your local authority

This is an underrated source of help and information. Many authorities employ advisers to help small businesses. These are especially useful on the subject of any grants available locally.

Many county library services are excellently organised to help the start-up businessman. The local business libraries will prove to be a particularly useful source of information for your market research. Consult the librarian.

Your accountant

Every business needs help in dealing with annual taxation. Beyond this, a businessman's accountant should be one of his chief sources of advice. But, as in all professions and trades, there are the good and the bad. Choose your accountant carefully, asking for recommendations from trustworthy sources. Don't just use the Yellow Pages.

Some accountants are mere historians, working out what you have made in the past, but of little help in planning for the future. If your accountant is capable of being your financial adviser as well as doing your books, you may consider yourself fortunate.

The time to consult your accountant is before you make a decision, or before you draw up your plan, not afterwards. Let him help with your business plan and your cash flow forecast.

Your customers

Always talk with your customers. Do not hesitate to ask their advice (remembering, however, that their advice will not be unbiased).

You will have consulted as many potential customers as possible in assessing the market for your product, and your business plan will be built on what they told you. Do not neglect them as a source of information and assistance later.

Your suppliers

A major supplier has a vested interest in the success of your business. Listen to his advice – unless he is trying to sell you something you don't really want.

Remember, he can be a valuable source of trade gossip and information about your competitors.

The Small Firms Service

This is a government service, available to all small businesses. Every major centre has one, staffed by a whole range of people giving both general and specialised advice. There are experts in the fields of patents, exports, employment legislation, etc. There are also advisers with particular experience in different types of business, for example mechanical engineering or food retailing, and many others.

No fees are charged for the first two advisory sessions with the Small Firms Service, but a small charge is made thereafter.

To find out where your nearest branch is, dial the telephone operator and ask for Freefone Enterprise.

Your solicitor

You will need the services of a solicitor for buying or selling property and for drawing up leases. A good commercial solicitor should also be asked to advise on service contracts and other matters involving legal considerations. As in other professions, specialisation is increasing among lawyers too, and the solicitor who dealt so well and tactfully with, say, a friend's divorce is not necessarily expert in company law or patent legislation. Choose carefully.

Insurance brokers

Consult an insurance broker before signing up with any one insurance company. Insurance is a competitive business these days, and a good broker, not bound to any one insurance company, can give sound advice.

Estate agents and surveyors

If you are looking for property, do not buy or lease the first you are offered. Shop around. When you find one that suits, get a good, independent surveyor to vet the property for you.

Other sources of business information and training

Courses in business training and skills, run by:

1. Local authorities
2. The Manpower Services Commission
3. Local Colleges of Further Education
4. 'Open Learning' establishments.

Some of these courses are well worth attending as you plan the start-up or expansion of your business. Addresses can be obtained from your local Enterprise Agency.

Business libraries
These can be found in most areas. The libraries run by county councils have been mentioned. More comprehensive business libraries can be found in the business schools and universities.

Books
A great many books have been published, most of them very specialised, which deal with all aspects of business.

Your attention is drawn to two in particular:

The first is a paperback, brief and well devised, written by Peter Hingston and entitled *The Greatest Little Business Book.*

The second, produced by the Macclesfield Business Ventures team, is *The Small Business Action Kit* (published by Kogan Page). It contains a series of short articles, checklists and tables intended to cover all aspects of small business. You are certain to find it useful.

Many of the pamphlets and brochures issued by banks and large firms of accountants also contain information of use to the small businessman.

Further reading from Kogan Page

Kogan Page publishes an extensive list of books for business managers and business owners; those particularly helpful to the reader of this book are likely to be:

The Business Plan Workbook, Colin and Paul Barrow, 1988
Buying for Business: How to Get the Best Deal from Your Suppliers, Tony Attwood, 1988
Debt Collection Made Easy, Peter Buckland, 1987
Financial Management for the Small Business, Colin Barrow, 2nd edition, 1988
How to Cut Your Business Costs, Peter D Brunt, 1988
How to Deal With Your Bank Manager, Geoffrey Sales, 1988
Profits from Improved Productivity, Fiona Halse and John Humphrey, 1988